THE SEVEN STEPS

TO

AWAKENING

by

Bhagavan Sri Ramana Maharshi

Sri Nisargadatta Maharaj

Sri Annamalai Swami

Sri Muruganar

Sri Sadhu Om

Sri Vasistha

Sri Sankara

Introduction, typesetting and text editing © 2010
The Freedom Religion Press

www.thefreedomreligionpress.com

www.seeseer.com

ISBN-13: 978-0-9797267-6-7

ISBN-10: 0-9797267-6-X

CONTENTS

INTRODUCTION

You, dear reader, have a choice. Choice A is to bring the impostor self and all forms of suffering to a final end and thus enjoy the perfect Awareness-Love-Bliss of your true Self forever.

Choice B is to continue to be controlled by the impostor self; identified with a temporary physical body that is subject to hundreds of diseases while living in a world that has had more than fifteen thousand wars in the last five thousand years.

As soon as there is any mention of bringing the impostor self to a final end, the impostor self in most humans immediately begins to generate thoughts, concepts and reasons for why the impostor self should not be brought to a final end.

The impostor self is very cunning and can use thoughts in thousands of different combinations to prevent you from bringing it to a final end. There are almost no spiritual teachings that effectively deal with the problem of the cunning tricks of the impostor self and thus almost no humans succeed in bringing the impostor self to a final end. Therefore it is essential to begin by facing the fact that almost no human really wants to bring the impostor self to a final end.

Why would anyone want to bring the impostor self to a final end? Because the true Self has never experienced any suffering in all eternity. The true Self is Infinite-Eternal-Awareness-Love-Bliss.

4

Eternal-Awareness-Love-Bliss is an infinitely better choice than being controlled by an impostor self that pretends to be you, but is not really you.

Some teachings call the impostor self "ego." Other teachings call the impostor self "mind." The term "impostor self" is a better term than "ego" because the word ego has so many different definitions. Psychology defines ego in one way, the dictionary defines ego in another way and these definitions are not the same as what the awakened sages mean by the word "ego."

The impostor self is thought. The impostor self is the words in your mind. Those words of the language or languages you are fluent in came from outside of you. That is why you cannot speak fluently in one hundred languages, because language comes from the outside. You existed before you learned the languages you now think in. Therefore you are not thought. However, thought pretends to be you.

One reason to make choice A is so that you can experience your true Self. In other words choice A is a choice to end the false and eternally live in the True.

The most effective means to stop the tricks of the impostor self is to increase your desire for liberation. The desire for liberation is the desire for freedom from:

1. The impostor self.

2. This false dreamlike world.

3. All forms of suffering.

The desire for liberation is also the desire to live as the true Self so that you can enjoy Awareness-Love-Bliss forever.

The importance of increasing your desire for liberation has been pointed out by many awakened sages such as Sri Nisargadatta Maharaj and Sri Sankara.

The question is how to make your desire for liberation increase? There are positive and negative ways to increase your desire for liberation. In *The Seven Steps to Awakening* one of the categories quotes have been placed under is Step Five; "Be inspired, encouraged and motivated to actually practice all seven steps." Reading those quotes repeatedly is a positive way to increase your desire for liberation. All of the quotes in *The Seven Steps to Awakening* have the potential to increase your desire for liberation.

Facing the negative aspects of the life the impostor self leads is a negative way to increase your desire for liberation. Comparing choice A with choice B is also a way to increase your desire for liberation.

When the desire for liberation becomes extremely intense:

1.   Self honesty becomes intense.

2.   Suddenly you can see the thousands of ways the impostor self tricked you in the past.

3.   Suddenly you see the significance of the quotes that the false self never allowed you to see before.

Historically, not even one in a million humans have succeeded in bringing the impostor self to its final end. That is because of the cunning tricks the impostor self uses to preserve its imaginary self. Those cunning tricks are mostly in the form of thoughts, concepts, ideas, desires, emotions, etc. Some of the quotes in *The Seven Steps to Awakening* were selected for the purpose of helping you to put an end to the tricks (preservation strategies) that the impostor self uses.

Some of the quotes in *The Seven Steps to Awakening* were selected to help put you back on track when the impostor self derails you from your journey to Awakening.

When one who is not free from the impostor self selects quotes, usually many of the quotes they select are quotes that will help the impostor self to continue. Even if they select some of the most powerful quotes, the impostor self does not let them see the significance of the quotes. Increasing your desire for liberation will help you to see the significance of the quotes and why the specific quotes in *The Seven Steps to Awakening* were selected.

Most people tend to think that everything an Awakened Sage says is a part of his or her teaching and therefore helpful for awakening. This is *not* true as the following saying of Sri Ramana Maharshi illustrates:

"The sage's pure mind which beholds as a mere witness the whole world is like a mirror which reflects the foolish thoughts of those who come before him. And these thoughts are then mistaken to be his."

That quote comes from the book *The Garland of Guru's Sayings* translated into English by K. Swaminathan. It is Garland quote number 1106. In *The Seven Steps to Awakening* it is quote number 34.

Thousands of pages of quotes have been printed because of the mistaken view that everything a sage says is a part of his or her teachings. Garland quote number 1106 corrects that mistaken view.

The quotes in *The Seven Steps to Awakening* are a loving transmission from your true Self. Through these quotes your true Self is communicating to you:

"I really love you and want the best for you. I don't want you to continue to suffer needlessly. Here in these quotes I am showing you the way to bring the illusion to an end and to awaken into the Reality of Eternal-Awareness-Love-Bliss. Here in these quotes I am showing you what most aspirants cannot see, even if they have read some of these quotes before. Here I have collected the quotes that are most essential and most helpful for those who really wish to awaken in this lifetime. Here I have collected the quotes that have no detours or distractions. Here I have collected the quotes that reveal the most direct means that brings the impostor self to its final end."

The quotes have been placed in various categories that are steps to awakening. The categories have been selected to be most helpful to show how to remove the obstacles that prevent most aspirants from bringing the impostor self to its final end.

The first step is to know that a journey that never goes beyond thought is *not* a journey to Awakening. Know the difference between:

A. Using the teachings as practice instructions.

B. Getting lost or stuck in concepts.

People often study spiritual teachings just because they find the concepts interesting. They like to discuss the teachings, argue about the teachings, think about the teachings, go on and on asking questions but missing answers, etc. Most people fail to distinguish between that which is essential and that which is merely a distraction or detour, like a group of people who meet in an automobile once per week to discuss various maps without ever putting the key in the ignition and without ever moving the car even one inch. Approaching the teachings this way assures failure to Awaken. Most people approach the teachings this way and most people fail to bring the impostor self to its final end.

In most people the desire to allow the impostor self to continue is much greater than their desire for liberation. Until that problem is honestly faced and corrected the impostor self will create many preservation strategies such as: 1. Distorting the teachings. 2. Choosing teachings that are not effective. 3. Avoiding the practice that leads to the impostor self's final end. 4. Staying in the realm of concepts. 5. Pretending to its imaginary self that it is not engaged in preservation strategies, etc. The impostor self directs the study of the teachings in a way that will insure that the impostor self can continue its imaginary existence.

When Sri Ramana Maharshi was in his teens a spontaneous experience came upon him that removed the impostor self from him forever. Sri Ramana Maharshi's body passed away in 1950.

Sri Muruganar was liberated from the impostor self soon after meeting Sri Ramana Maharshi. Sri Muruganar spent decades in the company of Sri Ramana Maharshi. Because Sri Muruganar was a liberated sage while collecting Sri Ramana Maharshi's sayings, *The Garland of Guru's Sayings* is the best source of Sri Ramana Maharshi's teachings. When the teachings are seen through the eyes of one who is not free from the impostor self, the teachings are distorted. Since Sri Muruganar was free from the impostor self while collecting Sri Ramana Maharshi's sayings, the teachings were seen clearly.

All of the Sri Ramana Maharshi quotes in *The Seven Steps to Awakening* come from K. Swaminathan's English translation of *The Garland of Guru's Sayings*. While probably not the most literal, it is the best translation for sincere aspirants who are truly dedicated to being liberated in this lifetime. It is a divinely inspired translation.

The intellectual and scholarly type of people tend to prefer the most literal translations. The intellectual and scholarly type of people almost never become free of the impostor self unless they cease to be the intellectual and scholarly type. The motivations of the sincere aspirant and the motivations of the intellectual and scholarly people are almost always quite different.

Not only avoiding arguing about spiritual teachings, but even avoiding the company of those who do spend time arguing about spiritual teachings has been advised by Sri Ramana Maharshi and other sages. Most people who consider themselves to be "devotees" do not even attempt to follow the advice given and that is an example of one of the impostor self's many tricks.

The Sri Muruganar quotes in *The Seven Steps to Awakening* come from the book *Sri Guru Ramana Prasadam* translated into English by Robert Butler.

Sri Sadhu Om spent many years in the company of Sri Ramana Maharshi and decades in the company of Sri Muruganar. The Sri Sadhu Om quotes in *The Seven Steps to Awakening* come from the book *The Path of Sri Ramana, Part One*. *The Path of Sri Ramana, Part One* is available as a free e-book at happinessofbeing.com. Many pages in *The Path of Sri Ramana, Part One* are devoted to explaining why Self-inquiry is really Self-attention. Here is a quote by Sri Sadhu Om: "In Sanskrit, the terms 'atman' and 'aham' both mean 'I'. Hence, 'atma-vichara' means an attention seeking 'Who is this I?' It may rather be called 'I-attention', 'Self-attention' or 'Self-abidance.'"

Often English translations of these teachings have so many non-English words that the book becomes a foreign language course instead of a spiritual teaching. The quotes in *The Seven Steps to Awakening* contain almost no non-English words. This was accomplished by selecting quotes that contain only English words, with a few exceptions such as the words *Guru* and *Yoga* which are already familiar to most English readers.

In the book *The Supreme Yoga* Swami Venkatesananda writes the following two definitions of the word vichara:

1.   "Vicara or inquiry is not reasoning nor analysis: it is directly looking into oneself."

2.   "Vicara, usually translated 'inquiry' is direct observation."

The spiritual meaning of the term "Self-inquiry" is directly looking into one's Self, which can also be described as Self-attention.   Since the true Self is awareness, this can also be described as attention to Awareness or Awareness aware of itself. This is *not* two awarenesses, one watching the other. This is just *one* Awareness aware of itself. And what is itself? Itself is Awareness. Thus, Awareness of Awareness. Directly looking into one's Self is directly looking into Awareness because the Self is Awareness. Sometimes the quotes refer to "Self-knowledge." "Self-knowledge" in these teachings does *not* mean conceptual knowledge. "Self-Awareness" or "Self-Experience" are closer to the spiritual meaning. When the quotes are warning against false knowledge, the word "knowledge" *does* mean conceptual knowledge.

Sri Annamalai Swami spent many years in the company of Sri Ramana Maharshi. Sri Annamalai Swami said that his years of constant meditation in the 1950's and 1960's finally brought him to a continuous awareness of the Self. The Sri Annamalai Swami quotes in *The Seven Steps to Awakening* come from the book *Annamalai Swami Final Talks*.

Sri Nisargadatta Maharaj's Guru told him to focus his attention on the 'I am' to the exclusion of all else. Sri Nisargadatta spent all of his free time doing that and after three years he realized the Self. The Sri Nisargadatta Maharaj quotes in *The Seven Steps to Awakening* come from the book *I AM THAT*.

Sri Sankara was one of the most prominent teachers in what the West calls "Hinduism." Some scholars say that Sri Sankara lived from 788 to 820 CE. The Sri Sankara quotes in *The Seven Steps to Awakening* are from *The Crest Jewel of Wisdom*. Some of the quotes are from Charles Johnston's English translation. Other quotes are from John Richard's English translation.

The *Yoga Vasistha* is an ancient scripture from what the West calls "Hinduism." Swami Venkatesananda's English translation of the *Yoga Vasistha* was published in 1976 under the title *The Supreme Yoga*.

Self honesty and a great increase in your desire for liberation are the two great keys that can make you one of the very few who succeed at bringing the impostor self to its final end.

If the direct practice that brings the impostor self to its final end is not clear to you from reading the quotes in *The Seven Steps to Awakening*, then you might consider reading the book *The Most Direct Means to Eternal Bliss*. There is a link on the www.seeseer.com website to where you can purchase *The Most Direct Means to Eternal Bliss*.

In the book *The Most Direct Means to Eternal Bliss* there are detailed descriptions of:

1.   The Awareness Watching Awareness practice.

2.   How to awaken the extremely intense desire for liberation.

3.   What the impostor self is and much more.

The Seven Steps to Awakening and *The Most Direct Means to Eternal Bliss* are two books that work very well together.

The teachings of Sri Ramana Maharshi, Sri Nisargadatta Maharaj and Sri Vasistha have a huge number of contradictions. The quotes selected for *The Seven Steps to Awakening* have kept the contradictions to a minimum. The quotes selected for *The Seven Steps to Awakening* are like a seamless unity that work very well together. The quotes selected for *The Seven Steps to Awakening* are helpful to all humans regardless of which spiritual path they are on.

HOW TO READ THE QUOTES

Read the quotes *very slowly*. Read *every* quote at least three times *before* going on to the next quote. Those who are very serious about awakening in this lifetime will read the quotes hundreds of times.

After you read a quote ask yourself these two questions:

A.   "What is the purpose of this quote?"

B.   "What would I have to do to put this purpose into practice?"

Ask those questions with *every* quote and then take the time to answer those questions. Write the answers down on paper and then read what you have written many times repeatedly. Or make an audio recording of your answers and play them back and listen to them many times repeatedly.

Use a highlighter pen to circle or underline the quotes you find most helpful. Then go back and read those quotes hundreds of times very slowly.

After reading all of the quotes, read all of the quotes in the book again very slowly. As your awareness expands you may be able to see great value in some of the quotes that you did not see great value in before.

The quotes in *The Seven Steps to Awakening* reveal the detours to be avoided and the direct path to take. The quotes in *The Seven Steps to Awakening* are practice instructions. The quotes in *The Seven Steps to Awakening* are doorways to Liberation. Liberation is eternal bliss and love, free from all forms of suffering.

Wishing you success in receiving the transmission.

STEP ONE

Know that a journey that never goes beyond words, ideas, thoughts or concepts is **not** *a journey to awakening.*

Know the difference between A. The final direct experience of infinite consciousness where all suffering, the body, the universe, etc. disappear forever and only infinite-eternal-awareness-love-bliss remains. B. Thinking about infinite consciousness or any other spiritual topic.
Thinking is **not** *Liberation or Realization.*

Know the difference between:

A. Using the teachings as practice instructions.

B. Getting lost or stuck in concepts.

The words and concepts taught in The Seven Steps to Awakening lead to the final awakening **only** *if they are actually practiced.*

Every *time you read a quote in The Seven Steps to Awakening ask yourself these two questions:*

A.   "What is the purpose of this quote?"

B.   "What would I have to do to put this purpose into practice?"

Write your answers to those questions or make an audio recording of your answers and play them back many times repeatedly. Then actually practice the teachings.

SRI RAMANA MAHARSHI

(1 – 40)

1.   Why do people call me learned? What is the mark of real learning? Learning that all garnered knowledge of things is empty ignorance and that true knowledge is the search for the Knower.

2.   Those who, learning to forget completely all objective knowledge, turn inward firmly and see clearly the truth, abide serene. Those who try to recall forgotten things pine bewildered, fretting over false phenomena.

3.   When knowledge marred by doubt and error disappears in true Awareness clear and pure, one thus established firmly in Self-Being, free from falsehood, has crossed over to the further shore of the river of knowledge.

4.   Even the knowledge sense-perceived of the world without has for its ground the Self above. To search for knowledge somewhere else apart from That is but to grasp the shadow, not the substance.

5.   Whatever notion may arise, never to let it live or grow, but to turn it that very instant, firm and stern, back to its source and merge it there, this is robust, intense detachment.

6.   Many are the ills that flow from mixing with mad folks afflicted with turbid minds and rattling tongues. Best friendship is with those good men whose minds are dead and who abide in the pure silence of awareness.

7.   Those who do not dive into the Heart and there confront the Self in the five sheaths hid are only students answering out of books clever questions raised by books, and not true seekers of the Self.

8.   The knowledge that ignores the Self, the knower, and holds as true the field perceived, is but illusive folly. No matter how much one has learned, true knowledge is the merging of all indicative knowledge in awareness of the Self.

9.   The one true light there is, is pure Awareness. Other kinds of knowledge clinging to it and claiming to be real are ego-born conceptual clouds. To trust them is sheer folly.

10.   All other kinds of knowledge are base, trivial. The only true and perfect knowledge is the stillness of pure awareness. The many differences perceived in the Self whose nature is awareness are wrong attributions and not real at all.

11.   What sort of knowledge is this wretched bodily-mental knowledge of objects? Would those who long for pure awareness hanker after this? To know pure awareness is true wisdom. All other knowledge is mere folly.

12.   What if one knows the subtle secret of manifold inscrutable mysteries? Until one knows the awareness which reveals all other knowledge, does one know the Truth?

13.   How can any treatise thrust some wisdom into that human-seeming heap of clay which keenly watches things perceived and not at all the Self, Awareness?

14.   What is worth seeking and discovering is the truth of Self. Such knowledge comes only to the still, clear intellect not muddled by strenuous search without but questing for the Truth in silence.

15.   "Of fate and effort, which is stronger? Which will yield? Which will prevail?" Those who wage this war of words are wholly ignorant of That from which the world and the ego both appear and into which they disappear.

16.   Some there are who endlessly jump and, sweating, shout full-throated refuting or elaborating doctrines instead of biding in clear silence inquiring into that which is and in the heart enjoying it.

17.   None can perceive the Sun, the Self, by arguments. Vexatious mental disputes are but conceits that cloud the light of truth and make the eyes in dizziness swim.

18.   Far from revealing Truth words only darken and conceal It. To let the Truth shine of itself instead of burying it in words; merge in the heart both word and thought.

19.   Let not your intellect become a slave to the mere sound and fury of controversy. Enter the heart with mind pellucid, concept-free, and realize your natural Being as the Truth.

20. From questing inward in the heart comes knowledge which destroys all false illusions.

21. Can hunger be appeased by eating food cooked over a painted flame? The end of pain, the bliss of peace results from egoless awareness, and not at all from verbal wisdom.

22. Never through argument, but only by abiding in the heart as pure awareness which lights up and shines within the mind, can one enjoy the thrill, the throb, the bliss supreme of being the Self.

23. Knowing aright the nature of the Self and abandoning the non-self as void, unreal, is wisdom true. All other knowledge is ignorance, and not wisdom.

24. Even like a dream this waking world is but a mind-conceived appearance in mind space. Hence greatness lies in firmly ending indicative knowledge and the folly of fondness for outer objects.

25. Knowledge is manifold, say they who know objects, but not freedom from the dire delusion of differences. When the senses five, driven outward by desire are pulled back, then true, full Awareness comes, and there is no "other" to be known.

26. Those whom from books have learnt about the truth supreme esteem themselves supreme in wisdom, and fail to seek the knower and taste the bliss of Self, but test and measure the silent sage. What folly this!

27. "Mine is the only mind amenable to my correction." If one forgets this truth and broods o'er others' faults one only fouls one's own mind more and more.

28. Only he who has attained immortal life can save the world. For the ignorant one to help another is but the blind leading the blind.

29. One has to blame oneself alone if one should try to teach the Truth supreme to those who are immature. These might reject the highest Truth as false because it contradicted what they had been told before and had believed as true.

30. As in the sky with thick clouds covered no eye can see the glorious sun, one fails to see one's own Self when the mind firmament is darkened by a dense cloud of thoughts.

31. For those whose mind has not completely subsided, the false knowledge theirs already has only served to pile up sorrows. Gaining more such so-called knowledge only deepens illusion's darkness, and helps not life at all.

32. While mind exists, creeds too exist. When mind turns inward in Self-quest and gets caught up in the heart, no creed can in that peace serene survive.

33. Being alone shines and rejoices as Awareness. Hence till all thought merges in absolute Being-Awareness, the poor conceptual mind can never know true Being, supreme Awareness.

34.   The sage's pure mind which beholds as a mere witness the whole world is like a mirror which reflects the foolish thoughts of those who come before him. And these thoughts are then mistaken to be his.

35.   The learned man who, letting go the Self, the real Being, sees and cherishes this dream, this false, illusive world, may be a scholar. Something different is he who has gained the clarity of Knowing the Self; he is a Knower.

36.   Holding in their hands the mirror, the scripture which declares "The Self alone is to be known", many alas, study with care the text and commentaries; only few seek the Self and gain true life.

37.   Far different from the scholar learned in books of wisdom is the Seer. Those who seek freedom from bondage of ignorance had better leave scholars alone and enter the presence of Seers established in the Self supreme.

38.   What is true religion? It is not speculating with that inconstant mind and endless speaking: "That is Being. No, that has no being. That has form. No, that is formless. That is non-dual. No, it is dual." It is the silence, the experience of deathless Being-Awareness-Bliss.

39.   In the language of duality alone are questions and answers. In non-duality they are not.

40.   He, who by questing inward for the Knower, has destroyed the ego and transcended so-called knowledge abides as the Self. He alone is a true knower, not one who has not seen the Self and therefore has an ego still.

SRI SADHU OM
(41 – 45)

41.   Thoughts are the enemy of happiness! Happiness reigns when thoughts subside! In fact, thoughts are the veil that covers over the happiness; when this veil is removed, happiness is revealed.

42.   Where thoughts cease, happiness reigns supreme; such is the truth about happiness. Although the thought-free state is gained and happiness is experienced for a while, such a thought-free state obtained by contact with external objects does not last long. Therefore, it is clear that one can never achieve the thought-free happy state permanently with the help of the five senses.

43.   However learned, rich or powerful he may be, if a man has no clear knowledge of what he really is, all his learning, greatness and power are merely fictitious! Hence, the first lesson to be learnt is about one's own Self.

44.   Whatever doubt may rise, it cannot rise without the rising of you – the first to have risen – who raised it. Therefore the primal doubt, namely that of not knowing who you are, is the root of all doubts!

45.   Until this primal doubt is cleared, replying to your other doubts will be just like cutting the leaves off the branches of a tree, because they will sprout again and again! But if the root is cut, they will not sprout again!

SRI MURUGANAR
(46 – 53)

46.   As the gracious light of inner realization entered my heart, all knowledge acquired through learning was exposed as merely a creation of the mind and as it fell away, my consciousness – free of attributes, shining in its natural state of attachment to the Self, that shines without attachment to anything – gained its final victory as the consciousness that is absolute and all-embracing.

47.   The Self abides as the fullness of consciousness within the mind and it alone illumines as the mind. Therefore only the science of (knowing) the grace of the Self that shines as pure consciousness is true science. All other sciences are false.

48.   If we apprehend the non-dual reality it will be seen that, within the Self that shines in the heart as the pure knowledge that it is our duty to learn and know, all other forms of knowledge have come into being through the illusory play of the mind.

49.   Through the miracle of grace that penetrated me in the form of true all-embracing consciousness, so that the ghostly charade created by the evil ego was abolished, I perceived that there was nothing that I needed to learn through the intellect.

50.   The heart in which words and thoughts have subsided and which remains as the all-pervading reality in which there is no going, no coming, no contact with anything whatsoever, will overflow with the ambrosial clarity of the supreme.

51.   The practice of abidance in the Self is to firmly hold the mind in abeyance within the heart. It is not an act of thinking.

52.   The Self shines through its very nature as a beautiful radiance within the Heart, as all thought subsides. Realizing that the power of thought could never truly grasp it, you should abandon all such conceptualization.

53.   The enduring attainment is to become established in the Heart, abiding as the pure 'I', unruffled by the fierce gale whipped up by all the various branches of knowledge that are apprehended through the mind and senses, and cause us agitation.

54.   All the information the mind accumulates and all the experiences it collects are ignorance, false knowledge. Real knowledge cannot be found in the mind or in any external location.

55.   Don't be interested in the words that the mind is serving up for you. It is putting them there to tempt you into a stream of thoughts that will take you away from the Self. You have to ignore them all and focus on the light that is shining within you.

SRI NISARGADATTA MAHARAJ
(56 – 119)

56.   Those who know only scriptures know nothing. To know is to be. I know what I am talking about; it is not from reading, or hearsay.

57.   On the verbal level everything is relative. Absolutes should be experienced, not discussed.

58.   Truth is simple and open to all. Why do you complicate? Truth is loving and lovable.

59.   Give up all questions except one: 'Who am I?' After all, the only fact you are sure of is that you are. The 'I am' is certain. The 'I am this' is not. Struggle to find out what you are in reality.

60.   All these questions arise from your believing yourself to be a person. Go beyond the personal and see.

61.   The realized man knows what others merely hear, but don't experience.

62.   My stand I take where nothing is; words do not reach there, nor thoughts.

63.   The real is experienced in silence.

64.   Maharaj: Remember facts, forget opinions.

Questioner: What is a fact?

Maharaj: What is perceived in pure awareness, unaffected by desire and fear is fact.

65.   You must know your own true being as indomitable, fearless, ever victorious. Once you know with absolute certainty that nothing can trouble you but your own imagination, you come to disregard your desires and fears, concepts and ideas and live by truth alone.

66.   It is the earnestness that liberates and not the theory.

67.   Your sincerity will guide you. Devotion to the goal of freedom and perfection will make you abandon all theories and systems and live by wisdom, intelligence and active love. Theories may be good as starting points, but must be abandoned, the sooner – the better.

68.   There is no need to turn round and round in endless questioning; find yourself and everything will fall into its proper place.

69.   Yours is a make-believe talk, all hangs on suppositions and assumptions. You speak with assurance about things you are not sure of.

70.   Words are of the mind and the mind obscures and distorts. Hence the absolute need to go beyond words and move over to my side.

71.   You give reality to concepts, while concepts are distortions of reality. Abandon all conceptualization and stay silent and attentive. Be earnest about it and all will be well with you.

72.   Try to go beyond the words.

73.   Unready means afraid. You are afraid of what you are. Your destination is the whole. But you are afraid that you will lose your identity. This is childishness, clinging to the toys, to your desires and fears, opinions and ideas. Give it all up and be ready for the real to assert itself.

74.   Do not worry about others. Deal with your own mind first.

75.   Learn to look without imagination, to listen without distortion.

76.   Your questions are about a non-existing person.

77.   The silence of the mind will dissolve and absorb all else.

78.   Do not ask superficial questions; apply yourself to fundamentals, to the very roots of your being.

79.   There are so many theories devised for explaining things – all are plausible, none is true.

80.   To see that all knowledge is a form of ignorance is itself a movement of reality.

81.   You want immediate results! We do not dispense magic here. Everybody does the same mistake: refusing the means, but wanting the ends.

82.   I cannot solve your problem by mere words. You have to act on what I told you and persevere. It is not right advice that liberates, but the action based on it.

83.   By doing you succeed, not by arguing.

84.   Now I know nothing, for all knowledge is in dream only and not valid.

85.   All experience is born of imagination; I do not imagine, so no birth or death happens to me.

86.   Let us not proceed by verbal logic.

87.   The most difficult are the intellectuals. They talk a lot, but are not serious.

88.   Merely talking about Reality without doing anything about it is self-defeating.

89.   You are entangled in the web of verbal definitions and formulations. Go beyond your concepts and ideas; in the silence of desire and thought the truth is found.

90.   Whatever is conceived by the mind must be false, for it is bound to be relative and limited.

91.   No university can teach you to be yourself. The only way to learn is by practice.

92.   You need to return to the state in which I am – your natural state. Anything else you may think of is an illusion and an obstacle.

93.   Stay beyond all thoughts, in silent being-awareness.

94.   The answer is not in words.

95.   Some events purify the mind and some stain it. Moments of deep insight and all-embracing love purify the mind, while desires and fears, envies and anger, blind beliefs and intellectual arrogance pollute and dull the psyche.

96.   All thinking is in duality. In identity no thought survives.

97.   Go forth, unburdened with ideas and beliefs. Abandon all verbal structures, all relative truth, all tangible objectives. The Absolute can be reached by absolute devotion only. Don't be half-hearted.

98.   Too much analysis leads you nowhere. There is in you the core of being which is beyond analysis, beyond the mind.

99.   Mere listening, even memorizing, is not enough. If you do not struggle hard to apply every word of it in your daily life, don't complain that you made no progress.

100.   Do understand that the mind has its limits; to go beyond, you must consent to silence.

101.   To see reality is as simple as to see one's face in a mirror. Only the mirror must be clear and true. A quiet mind, undistorted by desires and fears, free from ideas and opinions, clear on all the levels, is needed to reflect the reality.

102.   Realize that no ideas are your own; they all come to you from outside.

103.   Reality is not a concept, nor the manifestation of a concept. It has nothing to do with concepts.

104.   As the mind is made of words and images, so is every reflection in the mind. It covers up reality with verbalization and then complains.

105.   Questioner: How can I break through the barrier and know personally, intimately, what it means to be immutable?

Maharaj: The word itself is the bridge. Remember it, think of it, explore it, go round it, look at it from all directions, dive into it with earnest perseverance: endure all delays and disappointments till suddenly the mind turns round, away from the word, towards the reality beyond the word. It is like trying to find a person knowing his name only. A day comes when your inquiries bring you to him and the name becomes reality. Words are valuable, for between the word and its meaning there is a link and if one investigates the word assiduously, one crosses beyond the concept into the experience at the root of it. As a matter of fact, such repeated attempts to go beyond the words is what is called meditation.

106.   Be careful. The moment you start talking you create a verbal universe, a universe of words, ideas, concepts and abstractions, interwoven and interdependent, most wonderfully generating, supporting and explaining each other and yet all without essence or substance, mere creations of the mind. Words create words, reality is silent.

107.   Once you are beyond the person, you need no words.

108.   Words and questions come from the mind and hold you there. To go beyond the mind, you must be silent and quiet. Peace and silence; silence and peace – this is the way beyond. Stop asking questions.

109.   The words are most appropriate, but you do not grasp their full import. Go deep into the meaning of the words:

being, living, conscious,

and you will stop running in circles, asking questions, but missing answers.

110.   You need not know all the 'why' and 'how', there is no end to questions.

111.   Knowledge by the mind is not true knowledge.

112.   The idea that you know what is true is dangerous, for it keeps you imprisoned in the mind. It is when you do not know, that you are free to investigate.

113.   Words can only give you the idea and the idea is not the experience.

114.   It is earnestness that will take you through, not cleverness – your own or another's.

115.   There is no reality in ideas.

116.   As long as you have all sorts of ideas about yourself you know yourself through the mist of these ideas; to know yourself as you are, give up all ideas.

117.   Learning words is not enough. You may know the theory, but without the actual experience of yourself as the impersonal and unqualified center of being, love and bliss, mere verbal knowledge is sterile.

118.   So many words you have learnt, so many you have spoken. You know everything, but you do not know yourself. For the Self is not known through words – only direct insight will reveal it. Look within, search within.

119.   Whatever you can know with your mind is of the mind, not you.

THE SUPREME YOGA
(120 – 200)

120.   The fool asks irrelevant questions irreverently; and the greater fool is he who spurns the sage's wisdom. He is surely not a sage who responds to the vain questions of a foolish questioner.

121.   One should positively strive to enthrone wisdom in one's heart, for the mind is unsteady like a monkey. And, one should then avoid unwise company.

122.   Only he would wish to hear this who is ripe for liberation.

123.   Even as the ocean is the substratum of all the waves, direct experience is the basis for all proofs – the direct experience of truth as it is.

124.   Consciousness is pure, thought is subject to confusion.

125. People like to argue and confuse others; they are indeed confused.

126. All this discussion and argumentation take place only in and because of ignorance; when there is knowledge there is no duality. When the truth is known, all descriptions cease, and silence alone remains. Then you will realize that there is only one, without beginning and without end. But as long as words are used to denote a truth, duality is inevitable; however, such duality is not the truth. All divisions are illusory.

127. Ideas and experiences leave their mark on the mind which form the impressions or conditioning tendencies which are for the most part latent or dormant. But, when the mind is rid of these, the veil vanishes in a moment, like mist at sunrise, and with it the greatest sorrow also vanishes.

128. Conceptualization or imagination is productive of error and sorrow; and it can be so easily got rid of by Self-knowledge – and when it is got rid of there is great peace.

129. Ideas and thoughts are bondage; and their coming to an end is liberation.

130. Give up mental conditioning which alone is responsible for the perception of duality and remain totally unconditioned.

131. A painted pot of nectar is not nectar, nor a painted flame fire, and a painting of a woman is not a woman: wise words are mere words, not wisdom.

132. They who are established in the state of liberation, as pointed out by the scriptures, surely cross this ocean of world-appearance as their consciousness flows towards the Self. But, they who are caught in the net of polemics which are only productive of sorrow and confusion, forfeit their own highest good. Even in the case of the path shown by the scriptures, only one's direct experience leads one along the safest way to the supreme goal.

133. When you realize that which is indicated by the words, then naturally you will abandon the jugglery of words.

134. Give up notions, thoughts and intentions. When they cease, the mind naturally turns to what is truly beyond the mind – the infinite consciousness.

135. Ideation multiplies naturally by itself. This leads to sorrow, not to happiness.

136. Do not entertain ideas.

137. There is no cause for fear in the destruction of all ideation. When there is no thought, notion or ideation ceases.

138. When thus all notions cease, there is great peace, and sorrow is destroyed to its very root.

139.   Remove all thought: do not waste your life and effort in other endeavors.

140.   Bondage is bondage to thoughts and notions: freedom is freedom from them.

141.   There is no salvation without the total renunciation of all notions or ideas or mental conditioning.

142.   Though appearing to be intelligent, thought is unable to comprehend anything really.

143.   Craving is the root of all sorrow, and the only intelligent way is to renounce all cravings completely and not to indulge them. Even as fire burns all the more fiercely when fed with fuel, thoughts multiply by thinking: thoughts cease only by the extinction of thinking.

144.   Never again fall into the mire of conceptualization which is the cause of all sorrow.

145.   Do not be led astray by the long-winded empty statements of the wicked self-appointed teachers who have no direct experience.

146.   When consciousness abandons the perception of the three modes of time, when it is freed from the bondage of objectivity or conceptualization, it rests in utter tranquility.

147.   Because you are not fully enlightened your mind clings to the illusion of objective perception, of concepts.

148.   Mind is like a cloud of ignorance: dispel it by the repeated renunciation of all concepts and percepts.

149.   You have woven the web of your own concepts and are caught in it. If you can get rid of all that, attain purity, overcome even the fear of life and death and thus attain to total equanimity, you have achieved the greatest victory. On the other hand, if you cling to this ever-changing phenomenon called the world, you will surely perish in sorrow.

150.   The mind abandons everything when the vision of the supreme is gained. Hence, one should resolutely renounce everything till the supreme vision is gained. Not till one renounces everything is Self-knowledge gained: when all points of view are abandoned, what remains is the Self.

151.   At all times, everything is known only by direct experience.

152.   Just as a lamp utterly dispels darkness, the knowledge of truth completely uproots concepts and conditioning.

153.   If you conceptualize this teaching for your intellectual entertainment and do not let it act in your life, you will stumble and fall like a blind man.

154.   He in whom all concepts and habitual tendencies have ceased has overcome all mental conditioning and bondage.

155. Since the ignorant are bound fast to their own false notions, neither the transiency of the world nor the hard blow they suffer in their life is able to awaken them.

156. The truth or existence-consciousness-bliss absolute is beyond thought and understanding, it is supreme peace and omnipresent, it transcends imagination and description.

157. When non-dual being is known, the duality vanishes instantly. Belief (or imagination) gave rise to diversity; when that belief is dropped, diversity goes. Thought, imagination or belief gives rise to sorrow; to abandon such thinking is not painful! It is feeding these thoughts and beliefs that has brought about this sorrow; and this comes to an end by not entertaining those thoughts and beliefs.

158. All thoughts and beliefs lead to sorrow. Whereas no-thought and no-belief are pure bliss. Therefore, with the help of the fire of wisdom, vaporize the waters of your beliefs and become peaceful, supremely blissful. Behold the one infinite consciousness.

159. Objectification (or conceptualization) leads to Self-forgetfulness.

160. It is absolute truth and therefore not truth as a concept.

161. It is pure, absolute consciousness, naught else.

162.   Abandoning all limited concepts, abandoning even the division between the worshipper and the worshipped, worship the Self by the Self. Be at peace, pure, free from cravings.

163.   Conditioning is sorrow.   But conditioning is based on thoughts and notions. However, the truth is beyond such experience and the world is an appearance like a mirage!

164.   An imaginary object is imaginatively described by someone; and one understands in one's own imagination and imagines that he understands it.

165.   Abandoning mental conditioning, be a liberated soul.

166.   Ignorance and mental activity are perpetuated by each other.

167.   Remain for ever established in that state of utter freedom from movement of thought.

168.   Bhagiratha asked: I know that the Self alone is real and the body, etc. are not real. But how is it that it is not perfectly clear to me?

Tritala answered: Such intellectual knowledge is not knowledge!

169.   Vain argumentation is like boxing with space.

170. I shall instruct you if you are in a receptive mood and cherish my words. If one playfully instructs another merely in answer to a query, when the latter does not intend to receive, cherish and assimilate the teaching, it becomes fruitless.

171. A notional existence ceases only by the dawn of right knowledge and the cessation of all notions. Since the notional existence is unreal it ceases naturally when the truth is realized.

172. Give up all your doubts. Resort to moral courage.

173. One's limited understanding and one's own notions are the cause of bondage, and liberation is their absence. Hence, abandon all notions.

174. The thought-free, notion-less state is the best.

175. You are deluded because you do not recollect repeatedly and frequently the truth concerning the infinite consciousness, but you partake of the poison of self-limitation and the consequent psychological conditioning.

176. As and when the perception of an object arises within you, meet it with the understanding "I am not this." Such ignorant perception will immediately cease. In fact, there is nothing to be known in all this: there is need only to get rid of confusion or deluded understanding. If this delusion is not repeatedly revived, it ceases to be. Whatever notion arises in you, even as movement arises in wind, realize that "I am not this" and thus deprive it of support.

177.   Thinking, mental conditioning and imagination are meaningless and are productive only of psychological distress. All the sorrows and misfortunes of life are rooted in and rest in sense-experience and thinking.

178.   The mind is like a forest in spring. It is so dense with very many notions and concepts that dense darkness prevails in it. On account of self-limitation or ignorance, people undergo countless experiences of pleasure and pain in this world.

179.   I was not silent because I could not answer but because silence is the only answer to your question.

180.   All verbal statements (whether they are verbose or brief, whether their purport is subtle or transcendental) are limited by logic, by duality and division.

181.   The supreme Self is free from all notions. Notions give rise to objects and when the notions are abandoned the objects cease to be.

182.   Do not fall into the net of duality and non-duality, etc. All such controversy and polemics only lead to sorrow and despair. When one pursues the unreal or impermanent, there is sorrow. When the conditioning of consciousness drops away, there is no sorrow even as in sleep there is no sorrow. The consciousness that abandons conditioning realizes its unconditioned nature. That is liberation.

183.   The total abandonment of all notions or ideas is liberation and such an abandonment is possible when the pursuit of pleasure is abandoned.

184.   To rest content with the knowledge gained from the scriptures, considering oneself to be enlightened is like the vain imagination of the born-blind.

185.   Do not get involved in notions of matter and mind for they are false. Rest in your own Self.

186.   Ignorance is not dispelled by half-knowledge, even as there is no relief from cold when one sits near a painting of fire.

187.   The ignorant engages himself in endless arguments.

188.   At the end of the world-cycle, all these objects of perception cease to be. The one Self which is consciousness alone remains, and this is indescribable, being beyond thought and description. Only the sage of Self-knowledge experiences this: others merely read these words.

189.   There is something wrong with the scholars.

190.   When all mental activity ceases, you are that which is.

191.   Since he had not engaged himself in the persistent practice of the teachings, his heart was not fully established in the supreme state.

192.   He is surely a fool who thinks "I know this and I have nothing more to know" after once reading this.

193.   Abandon the words but remain established in the experience of the truth they indicate.

194.   That supreme state is beyond all concepts.

195.   When one thoroughly investigates all this, it is clearly seen that the pure consciousness alone exists and nothing else. It is beyond description. At the end of the investigation utter silence alone remains.

196.   The truth does not become clear in you until it is heard again and again and meditated upon again and again.

197.   Enough of this confusing argumentation concerning unity and diversity.

198.   The hall-mark of enlightenment is cessation of craving. When the latter is absent, there is no enlightenment but scholasticity which is in fact ignorance or viciousness.

199.   This supreme truth is established only in total silence, not by logic, discussion and argumentation.

200.   Thus, O sage, it is clear that Self-knowledge is beyond the reach of the jugglery of words.

201. The veiling effect only disappears with full experience of Reality, and the elimination of false knowledge leads to the end of suffering caused by that distraction.

202. There is no such thing as ignorance beyond the thinking mind. Thought itself is ignorance, the cause of the bondage of becoming. When thought is eliminated, everything else is eliminated. When thought increases everything else increases.

203. While the scholar does not overcome his sense of 'I am this' in the body and its faculties, there is no liberation for him, however much he may be learned in religion and philosophy.

204. Reality can be experienced only with the eye of understanding, not just by a scholar. What the moon is like must be seen with one's own eyes. How can others do it for you?

205. Speech alone, even a deluge of words, with scholarship and skill in commenting on the scriptures, may achieve some personal satisfaction but not liberation.

206. The tangle of words is a great forest which leads the mind off wandering about, so wise men should strive to get to know the truth about their own nature.

207. In the silence is the highest peace because wavering is the intellect's unreal work; there the knowers of the Eternal, mighty-souled, enjoy unbroken happiness of partless bliss, recognizing the Self as the Eternal.

208. There is no higher cause of joy than silence where no mind-pictures dwell; it belongs to him who has understood the Self's own being; who is full of the essence of the bliss of the Self.

209. Through unwavering ecstasy is clearly understood the reality of the Eternal, fixed and sure. This cannot be when other thoughts are confused with it, by the motions of the mind.

210. Whose being neither intellect nor reason knows – this is the Eternal, THAT THOU ART.

211. Freedom is won by a perception of the Self's oneness with the Eternal, and not by the doctrines of Union or of Numbers, nor by rites and sciences.

212. An eloquent voice, a stream of words, skill in explaining the teaching, and the learning of the learned; these bring enjoyment but not freedom.

213. Through information, digging, and casting aside the stones, a treasure may be found, but not by calling it to come forth.

STEP TWO

Know that the world is a dreamlike illusion.

Know that all of the following are dreamlike illusions:
(a – f)

a.   *The world.*
b.   *The body.*
c.   *The universe.*
d.   *All dimensions.*
e.   *All events, motions and actions.*
f.   *Time.*

Almost all of the words in a dictionary describe dreamlike illusions.

SRI RAMANA MAHARSHI
(214 – 250)

214.   From your true being as Awareness alienated and deluded do not pursue appearances, deeming them as real.   They are false, since disappear they must.   But your own being as Awareness is real and cannot cease to be.

215.   The world appears distinctly only in wakefulness and dream with concepts filled.   In concept-free, all empty sleep, one sees no world; so then conceptual is the world's whole substance.

216.   The mind bewildered which mistakes the body for oneself conceives the transient world of names and forms, makes it seem real and lovable, and promptly entraps one in the strong, illusive bondage of desire.

217.   The empirical world of jostling names and forms is false and has no real existence in bright, full Awareness. Like a ring of fire formed in the dark when one whirls fast a glowing joss-stick, 'tis an illusion, mind-created.

218.   One ever-present pure Awareness, this alone has true existence. The world perceived and measured by you is but illusion, jaundiced yellow, caused by the ego's concepts false and treacherous desires.

219.   Seen in the light of Self-experience all this phenomenal world is mere appearance, like the sky's deep blueness. What the deluded, body-bound ego perceives 'out there' is mind-created, nothing more.

220.   This villainous vast world so false that cheats and churns the minds of all, how did it come to be? By nothing else but by the fault of falling from the Self instead of clinging firmly to It.

221.   The world, like snake in rope, thief in a stump, mirage in air, has no real existence. Seeming to be, mere appearance, is its nature.

222.   By this world That world is concealed. And this world is by That concealed. Names and forms one sees, or else one sees pure Being-Awareness-Bliss.

223. The world that hides the Self is but a dream. When the phenomenal world is hidden by the Self's bright light, Awareness pure, the Self, abides.

224. The nature of this mind-created world, now seen in dream-light dim, is truly known only in that bright Being-Awareness which transcends the mind's illusion.

225. Some assert, "This world before our eyes lacks permanence, 'tis true. But it is real while it lasts." We deny it saying, "Permanence is a criterion of Reality."

226. Some argue, "Though divisible and split up into parts, the world we know so well, how could it be unreal?" We refute it, saying, "Wholeness too is a criterion of Reality."

227. The wise can nohow deem as real a world divided and destroyed by time's wheel. Whole, eternal, perfect, ever-shining and transcending time and space, such is the nature of Reality.

228. The goings-on of the empirical world, true-seeming and beguiling in the mind's borrowed light, are nothing but illusions in the bright light of pure Awareness.

229. Only mad folk perplexed because they deem the false world to be real find joy in this illusion. The truly wise find joy in nothing but Awareness which is Being.

230.   What is the Self's self-transformation as the world?   A twist of straw appearing as a snake?   Look hard you see no snake at all.   There was no transformation, no creation, none, no world at all.

231.   Did the Self lapse from its own wholeness as Being, you ask, "How else did this world come to be?" It came from ignorance false.   The Self can never suffer any change at any time.

232.   Vast, whole, immutable, the Self reflected in the mind's distorting mirror may appear to move.   Know that it is the image moving, the true Self never moves or changes.

233.   How can the dark, delusive sense of separateness affect the Self which is non-dual?   It is the mind's divisive vision which sees difference.   Awareness knows no separateness at all.

234.   Those who forget the harm the false world there before us does, and cling to it as real and comfortable, mistake, alas, a floating bear for a boat only to be crushed and drowned in the sea of birth.

235.   When will the fool who thinks the body and the world are permanent and clings to them, find peace? Only when this folly leaves him and he trusts and like a limpet clings to that, the Self within.   Thenceforward he shall never more know pain.

236.   Only by courtesy is the body, vulnerable and born to die, called an entity substantial. The sole reality, the only thing permanent and ultimate, is Self-awareness, That alone.

237.   Know that these countless things are pictures in a dream and none is real apart from the beholder. Shun this phantom world of names and forms and dwell in the pure, blissful being of Awareness.

238.   O worldly folk who long for and run after an endless series of unenduring things, 'tis wisdom true to seek and know That one thing on knowing which all other things will cease to be.

239.   When the full identity is reached that the Self is all and there is no "other", the various perceptions rife in the absence of Self-inquiry and Self-abidance are all seen as mere mistakes.

240.   One forgets the Self and thinks the body is oneself and goes through innumerable births and in the end remembers and remains the Self. Know this is only like awaking from a dream wherein one has wandered all over the world.

241.   Seeing this mind-projected world in sheer delusion, then taking it as real, and swerving from the Truth sublime of one's own Being as pure Awareness, one but proves oneself insane.

242.   Destroying through discrimination the basic error that I am the body, an object, and rejecting it and the world as mere mirages false, the Awareness that surviving shines alone as Being, That am I.

243.   When one now deeming oneself the mind and wandering lost amid phenomena, wakes up from this dream-spectacle and remerges in the Self and stands as That, this is the inwardness of yoga true.

244.   The universe out there appears when scanned. But when not scanned, it disappears. Turning away from this, search keenly for the Self within the heart, and think no more of birth.

245.   Renouncing this phenomenal world which seems to, but does not exist, we gain the Self, the Awareness shining all unseen.

246.   Seen through the eye of our true being which is awareness pure, supreme, what we call "birth" is but the folly of thinking that one is the body which forms a poor part of this entirely false phenomenal world.

247.   Until the snake-illusion goes, its ground, the real rope, will not be recognized. Until the world of false phenomena disappears, the Self, its ground, will not shine clear.

248.   Only when the world-illusion goes does the blissful light of Self arrive. Life lived in this bright, blissful light is our true, natural life. Other ways of life are full of trouble and fear.

249. Is there a greater folly than the aching folly of supposing that the Self, the I of pure awareness which does not see this changing world at all, is subject to some change?

250. Pure Being, our Self-nature, That alone exists eternally. Apart from That, all objects we perceive are clusters of illusive appearances that come and go, while That, unmoving and unchanged, abides the same for ever.

SRI MURUGANAR
(251 – 261)

251. Absolute existence, the pure sky of grace free from the sorrow of 'I' and 'mine', will be attained when, in the mind that sees as the Self and has died in that supreme reality, the imaginary concepts of the world and the physical body have entirely ceased to be.

252. The eye of the Self, consciousness, alone constitutes true seeing. That eye never perceives anything at all. If it be said that the eye perceives anything whatsoever, then that eye too, like the thing it perceives, is a mental creation. It is not the true eye.

253. Know that the vision of the truth we behold when we enter and subside within the heart – so that the treacherous ties of worldly bondage that attend the illusion of the body are abolished – is indeed the gracious state of liberation.

254. In the heart, the Self that exists as the eye of grace, none of the worlds truly exist.

255. Ignorance will not be eradicated except in those who, through the power of Self-inquiry conducted assiduously within the heart, have attained the victorious absolute vision in which the whole panoply of manifestation is transcended, being seen as a mere cinema show.

256. The infinite variety of false and treacherous modes of existence are merely brightly colored images appearing as if in a mirror. We must realize that the false and treacherous identification of the 'I' with the body is the seed from which these appearances arise to ensnare us, and we must reject it with disdain.

257. It is indeed pitiable to spurn, forfeit and lose the treasure that consists in dwelling thought-free within the Heart, on account of the vacillating mind that dwells upon the world-dream generated by the treacherous senses, taking it to be real.

258. The Self, revealed as our true nature within the heart through the power of Self-inquiry, is none other than the peerless reality of the Supreme, which alone remains after this worldly illusion has faded into nothingness.

259. That which is spoken of as the Life of life itself is the true life. That other 'life' is merely the body. That illusory knowledge mediated by the senses is nothing but delusion. The pure consciousness that underlies it alone is true consciousness.

260.   The supreme reality – in which the noble nature of pure grace flourishes, and which merges with us so that all the many false appearances such as 'this birth' and 'the next birth' cease to exist – shines out as the truth-imbued and flawless 'I'.

261.   If I am to affirm who I am, my true nature, I am the Self that knows nothing of the fleshly body, life, intelligence and mind, that is free of all darkness, the true 'I' that excels as pure consciousness.

SRI ANNAMALAI SWAMI
(262 – 270)

262.   Mind and body are like the tongue and teeth in the mouth. They have to work in harmony with each other. The teeth do not fight with the tongue and bite it. Mind and body should combine in the same harmonious way.   However, if we want to go beyond the body, beyond the mind, we have to understand and fully accept that all the information the senses provide is not real. Like the mirage that produces an illusory oasis in the desert, the senses create the impression that there is a real world in front of us that is being perceived by the mind. The apparent reality of the world is an illusion. It is merely a misperception. When the mind perceives a snake where in reality there is only a rope, this is clearly a case of the senses projecting an imaginary image unto a real substratum. This, on a much larger scale, is how the unreal appearance of the world is projected by the

mind and the senses unto the underlying reality of the Self.

Once this happens, we see the superimposition, the unreal names and forms we have created, and we forget about the substratum, the reality that underlies them.

263.   We think we live in a real, materially substantial world, and that our minds and bodies are real entities that move around in it.   When the Self is seen and known, all these false ideas fade away and one is left with the knowledge: Self alone exists.

264.   There are dream consequences for the bad acts committed in the dream, and while you still take the dream to be the reality, you will suffer the consequences of your bad behavior.   Do no evil and have no hate. Have equanimity towards everything.

265.   Since the Self is infinite and immaterial, what it 'sees' is infinite and immaterial.

266.   Bad thoughts make bad dreams and good thoughts make good dreams, and if you have no thoughts you don't dream at all.

267.   Your real state is the Self, and in that Self there is no body and no mind.

268.   This life is all a dream, a dream within a dream. We dream this world, we dream that we die and take birth in another body. And in this birth we dream that we have dreams. All kinds of pleasures and suffering alternate in these dreams, but a moment comes when waking up happens. In this moment, which we call realizing the Self, there is the understanding that all the births, all the deaths, all the sufferings and all the pleasures were unreal dreams that have finally come to an end.

269.   You are looking for satisfaction in the outside world because you think that all these objects you see in front of you are real. They are not.

270.   If you abide as the Self, you will see the world as the Self. In fact, there will be no world at all.

SRI NISARGADATTA MAHARAJ
(271 – 316)

271.   What do you know of me, when even my talk with you is in your world only?

272.   Questioner: Is your world full of things and people as is mine?

Maharaj: No, it is full of myself.

273.   The world you can perceive is a very small world indeed. And it is entirely private. Take it to be a dream and be done with it.

274.   However long a life may be, it is but a moment and a dream.

275.   In reality only the Ultimate is. The rest is a matter of name and form. And as long as you cling to the idea that only what has name and shape exists, the Supreme will appear to you non-existing. When you understand that names and shapes are hollow shells without any content whatsoever, and what is real is nameless and formless, pure energy of life and light of consciousness, you will be at peace – immersed in the deep silence of reality.

276.   To take appearance for reality is a grievous sin and the cause of all calamities.

277.   Within the prison of your world appears a man who tells you that the world of painful contradictions, which you have created, is neither continuous nor permanent and is based on a misapprehension. He pleads with you to get out of it, by the same way by which you got into it. You got into it by forgetting what you are and you will get out of it by knowing yourself as you are.

278.   When you shall begin to question your dream, awakening will be not far away.

279.   Your world is transient, changeful. My world is perfect, changeless.

280.   In my world nothing happens.

281.   Maharaj: My world is real, while yours is made of dreams.

Questioner: Yet we are talking.

Maharaj: The talk is in your world. In mine – there is eternal silence. My silence sings, my emptiness is full, I lack nothing. You cannot know my world until you are there.

282.   Your mistake lies in your belief that you are born. You were never born nor will you ever die, but you believe that you were born at a certain date and place and that a particular body is your own.

283.   It is in the nature of desire to prompt the mind to create a world for its fulfillment.

284.   Desire can produce a universe; its powers are miraculous.

285.   In reality nothing ever happens.

286.   The only thing that can help is to wake up from the dream.

287.   Treating everything as a dream liberates. As long as you give reality to dreams, you are their slave. By imagining that you are born as so-and-so, you become a slave to the so-and-so.

288.   Only reality is, there is nothing else. The three states of waking, dreaming and sleeping are not me and I am not in them.

289.   The main point to grasp is that you have projected unto yourself a world of your own imagination, based on memories, on desires and fears, and that you have imprisoned yourself in it. Break the spell and be free.

290.   Stop attributing names and shapes to the essentially nameless and formless, realize that every mode of perception is subjective, that what is seen or heard, touched or smelt, felt or thought, expected or imagined, is in the mind and not in reality, and you will experience peace and freedom from fear.

291.   You cannot be rid of problems without abandoning illusions.

292.   Truth is permanent. The real is changeless. What changes is not real, what is real does not change.

293.   He who knows the state in which there is neither the world nor the thought of it, he is the Supreme Teacher.

294.   In pure consciousness nothing ever happens.

295.   The real does not die, the unreal never lived.

296.   You are neither the body nor in the body – there is no such thing as body.   You have grievously misunderstood yourself; to understand rightly – investigate.

297.   My heart wants you awake. I see you suffer in your dream and I know that you must wake up to end your woes. When you see your dream as dream, you wake up. But in your dream itself I am not interested. Enough for me to know that you must wake up.

298.   Do not be misled by my eating and smoking, reading and talking. My mind is not here, my life is not here. Your world, of desires and their fulfillments, of fears and their escapes, is definitely not my world. I do not even perceive it.

299.   Without imagination there is no world.

300.   The moment you allow your imagination to spin, it at once spins out a universe. It is not at all as you imagine and I am not bound by your imaginings.

301.   The intelligence and power are all used up in your imagination. It has absorbed you so completely that you just cannot grasp how far from reality you have wandered.   No doubt imagination is richly creative. Universe within universe are built on it. Yet they are all in space and time, past and future, which just do not exist.

302.   Maharaj: This body appears in your mind; in my mind nothing is.

Questioner: Do you mean to say you are quite unconscious of having a body?

Maharaj: On the contrary, I am conscious of not having a body.

Questioner: I see you smoking!

Maharaj: Exactly so. You see me smoking. Find out for yourself how did you come to see me smoking, and you will easily realize that it is your 'I-am-the-body' state of mind that is responsible for this 'I-see-you-smoking' idea.

303.   Questioner: If all that passes has no being, then the universe has no being either.

Maharaj: Who ever denies it? Of course the universe has no being.

304.   I am offering you exactly what you need – awakening.

305.   Engrossed in a dream you have forgotten your true Self.

306.   Nothing dies. The body is just imagined. There is no such thing.

307. There is no body, nor a world to contain it; there is only a mental condition, a dreamlike state, easy to dispel by questioning its reality.

308. I am trying to wake you up, whatever your dream.

309. It is by your consent that the world exists. Withdraw your belief in its reality and it will dissolve like a dream.

310. Cease from looking for happiness and reality in a dream and you will wake up.

311. The world cannot give what it does not have; unreal to the core, it is of no use for real happiness. It cannot be otherwise. We seek the real because we are unhappy with the unreal. Happiness is our real nature and we shall never rest until we find it. But rarely we know where to seek it. Once you have understood that the world is but a mistaken view of reality, and is not what it appears to be, you are free of its obsessions. Only what is compatible with your real being can make you happy; and the world, as you perceive it, is its outright denial.

312. Do understand that what you think to be the world is your own mind.

313.   Once you have seen that you are dreaming, you shall wake up. But you do not see, because you want the dream to continue. A day will come when you will long for the ending of the dream, with all your heart and mind, and be willing to pay any price; the price will be dispassion and detachment, the loss of interest in the dream itself.

314.   I do not need the world. Nor am I in one.

315.   However great and complete is your world, it is self-contradictory and transitory and altogether illusory.

316.   If you seek real happiness, unassailable and unchangeable, you must leave the world with its pains and pleasures behind you.

THE SUPREME YOGA
(317 – 511)

317.   Neither freedom from sorrow nor realization of one's real nature is possible as long as the conviction does not arise in one that the world-appearance is unreal.

318.   All enjoyments in this world are deluded, like the lunatic's enjoyment of the taste of fruits reflected in a mirror. All the hopes of man in this world are consistently destroyed by time.

319.   In this world there is nothing, high or low, that time does not destroy.

320.   Neither the world of matter nor the modes of creation are truly real; yet the living and the dead think and feel they are real. Ignorance of this truth keeps up the appearance.

321.   As long as the highest wisdom does not dawn in the heart, the person revolves in this wheel of birth and death.

322.   The materiality of the creation is like the castle in the air, an illusory projection of one's own mind – imaginary.

323.   When this notion of the object is firmly rejected and removed from the subject, then consciousness alone exists without even an apparent or potential objectivity.

324.   The wrong notion that this world is real has become deep rooted on account of persistent wrong thinking.

325.   What is known as liberation is indeed the absolute itself, which alone is. That which is perceived here as 'I', 'you' etc., only seems to be, for it has never been created.

326.   In truth, this world does not arise from the absolute nor does it merge in it. The absolute alone exists now and for ever.

327.   All this is mere imagination or thought. Even now nothing has ever been created; the pure infinite space alone exists.

328.   Cosmic consciousness alone exists now and ever; in it are no worlds, no created beings.

329.   Even as an unreal nightmare produces real results, this world seems to give rise to a sense of reality in a state of ignorance. When true wisdom arises, this unreality vanishes.

330.   Changes in the unchanging are imagined by ignorant and deluded people.

331.   This world and this creation is nothing but memory, dream: distance, measures of time like a moment and an age, all these are hallucinations.

332.   Liberation is the realization of the total non-existence of the universe as such. This is different from a mere denial of the existence of the ego and the universe! The latter is only half-knowledge.

333.   In dream, the dream-body appears to be real; but when there is an awakening to the fact of dream, the reality of that body vanishes. Even so, the physical body which is sustained by memory and latent tendencies is seen to be unreal when they are seen to be unreal.

334.   There is no universe, no distance, no barriers.

335.   It is the nature of appearance to appear to be real, even though it is unreal.

336.   In the mind of the deluded, the unreal manifests itself; and when the delusion has been dispelled there is no longer an ignorant fancy. This fanciful conviction that the unreal is real is deep-rooted by repeated imagination.

337.   The physical body is only the creation of one's ignorant fancy, not real.

338.   No creation takes place in the Supreme Being or the infinite consciousness; and the infinite consciousness is not involved in the creation.

339.   When there is notion of creation, the creation seems to be: and when, through self-effort, there is understanding of non-creation, there is no world.

340.   Even as liquor is able to make one see all sorts of phantasms in the empty sky, mind is able to make one see diversity in unity. Even as a drunkard sees a tree moving, the ignorant one sees movement in this world.

341.   When the mind entertains notions of objects, there is agitation or movement in the mind; and when there are no objects or ideas, then there is no movement of thought in the mind. When there is movement, the world appears to be; when there is no movement, there is cessation of world-appearance.

342. In truth, there is no creation, and hence no division at all.

343. When the world is assumed to be real, the Self is not seen: but when this assumption is discarded, consciousness is realized.

344. The seer alone is real, the object being hallucination.

345. When Self-knowledge arises and the object ceases to be, the seer is realized as the sole reality.

346. It is the mind that makes things appear here. It brings about the appearance of the body, etc., naught else is aware of the body.

347. The infinite consciousness alone IS.

348. Some arrive at this understanding soon, others after a very long time.

349. When we inquire into the nature of the mind, all the created objects or all appearances are seen to be its creations; only the infinite consciousness remains as uncreated by the mind.

350. The enlightened one knows that there is only one reality – the infinite consciousness.

351. This world is nothing but pure hallucination.

352.   The mind veils the real nature of the Self and creates an illusory appearance with many branches, flowers and fruits. Destroy this illusion by wisdom and rest in peace.

353.   The seed of this world-appearance is ignorance.

354.   It is only the limitation of thought that perceives the world-appearance.   This world-appearance is delusion: it is better not to let the very thought of it arise again in the mind.

355.   It is only in a state of ignorance that the mind dreams of the world-appearance, not when it is awake or enlightened.

356.   Such indeed is the nature of this utter ignorance, this delusion, and this world-process: without real existence there is this illusory notion of egotism. This egotism does not exist in the infinite Self. In the infinite Self there is no creator, no creation, no worlds, no heaven, no humans, no demons, no bodies, no elements, no time.

357.   There is no creation.   The infinite has never abandoned its infinity. THAT has never become this.

358.   The power of nescience is capable of creating a total confusion between the real and the unreal.

359.   Nescience and the Self cannot have any relationship.

360. Thought alone creates all these divisions and illusions. When it ceases, creation ceases.

361. Only as long as the delusion of this world-appearance lasts is there this existence of the world as an object of perception.

362. This world-appearance is experienced only like a day-dream; it is essentially unreal.

363. There is no cause and effect relation between the Supreme Being and the universe.

364. The world is not seen in the supreme non-dual consciousness.

365. Mind alone by its thinking faculty conjures up what is known as the body: no body is seen where the mind does not function!

366. It is the mind that creates the body with all its limbs. Mind itself is both the sentient and the insentient beings; all this endless diversity is nothing but mind.

367. It is the mind that 'creates' the body by mere thoughts.

368. The ignorant man with a gross physical vision sees the physical body as different from and independent of the mind.

369.   It is indeed true to say that there are no waves in the ocean; the ocean alone exists.

370.   The physical body is nothing but the fruit of the fancy of the mind; the physical body is not an existential fact independent of the mind.

371.   This world exists only in appearance or imagination and not because one sees the material substances. It is like a long dream or a juggler's trick.

372.   Each individual sees only those objects which are rooted in his own mind. When the ideas in the mind do not bear fruits, there is a change in the mind; there follows a succession of births to suit these psychological changes. It is this psychological connection that creates the conviction in the reality of birth and death and in the reality of the body. When this conviction is given up, there is the cessation of embodiment.

373.   The notions of 'I' and 'the world' are but shadows, not truth.

374.   He sees the truth who sees the body as a product of deluded understanding and as the fountain-source of misfortune; and who knows that the body is not the Self.

375.   He sees the truth who is not deluded into thinking that he is the body which is subject to illness, fear, agitation, old age and death.

376.   He sees the truth who knows that the Self alone exists and that there is no substance to objectivity.

377.   Mind alone is this universe.

378.   Consciousness reflecting in consciousness shines as consciousness and exists as consciousness; yet, to one who is ignorant, though considering oneself as wise and rational, there arises the notion that there has come into being and there exists something other than this consciousness.

379.   The mind alone is this world-appearance, this world appearance has arisen in it and it rests in the mind. When the objects as well as the experiencing mind have become tranquil, consciousness alone remains.

380.   There is no world in reality.

381.   All this creation takes place only as in a dream. This creation is not real; it merely appears to be so.

382.   These universes arise and vanish again and again. But these are different from the one infinite consciousness.

383.   All this is unreal, like the creations seen in a dream. Hence the question: "How did all this arise in the one infinite consciousness?" is immature and childish. The creation appears to take place on account of the intentions of the mind.

384.   This creation is nothing but the creation of the mind: this is the truth; the rest is but a fanciful description.

385. The repetition (creation and dissolution) of infinite number of universes, with the infinite variety of creators in them, is nothing but the fanciful perception of the ignorant and the deluded.

386. Your birth is unreal.

387. The Self is devoid of the senses.

388. That alone can be regarded as the truth which has always been and which will always be.

389. Mind alone is the seed for this delusion of world-appearance; it is the mind that gives rise to the false sense of "I" and "mine."

390. Nothing in this world is truly enduring.

391. What you see as the world is only an illusory appearance.

392. The Self is real, birth and death are imaginary.

393. I am the unborn in whom the world-appearance has vanished.

394. It is only in the eyes of the ignorant that even your form exists.

395. This cosmic illusion leads the unwary mind into endless difficulties.

396. When one is firmly established in Self-knowledge, which is infinite, unlimited and unconditioned, then the delusion or ignorance that gave rise to world-appearance comes to an end.

397. The sun and the worlds become non-objects of perception to them who have gone beyond the realm of objective perception and knowledge.

398. The ignorant man does not realize the unreality of the objects because he has not realized the reality.

399. When you have gained Self-knowledge and when your consciousness has infinitely expanded, your mind no longer falls into the cesspool of this world.

400. There is no way other than Self-knowledge for the cutting asunder of bondage and for crossing this ocean of illusion.

401. The supreme Self has no relationship with this world-appearance.

402. The ignorant person accepts as real whatever he sees in this world; not so the wise one. Even as a piece of wood and water in which it is reflected have no real relationship, the body and the Self have no real relationship.

403. This universe has been conjured up in empty space merely by mental conditioning: it is not a reality.

404. There is no duality; there are no bodies and therefore there are no relationships among them.

405. Be not deluded. Abandon false perception and behold the truth.

406. When the mind abandons the movement of thought, the appearance of the world-illusion ceases.

407. Caught up in his own conditioning, whatever the person sees, he thinks that to be real and gets deluded. And on account of the intensity of the conditioning and the fancy, he discards his own nature and perceives only the world-illusion.

408. This entire creation is pervaded by ignorance which sustains it.

409. Birth and childhood lead to youth; youth leads to old age; and old age ends in death – and all these are repeatedly experienced by the ignorant.

410. Nothing has really become physical or material.

411. That which has a beginning has an end. When all things that have a beginning are ruled out, what remains is the truth which is the cessation of ignorance.

412.   This house known as the body has not been made by anyone in fact! It is only an appearance, like the two moons seen by one suffering from diplopia. The moon is really only one; the duality is an optical illusion. The body is experienced to exist only when the notion of a physical body prevails in the mind; it is unreal.

413.   There are thousands of such bodies which have been brought into being by your thought-force.

414.   By continually entertaining notions such as "This is it.", "This is mine." and "This is my world." such notions assume the appearance of substantiality. The permanency of the world is also an illusion: in the dream-state what is really a brief moment is experienced by the dreamer as a lifetime. In a mirage only the illusory "water" is seen and not the substratum: even so, in a state of ignorance one sees only the illusory world-appearance but not the substratum. However, when one has shed that ignorance, the illusory appearance vanishes.

415.   For your spiritual awakening I declare again and again: this world-appearance is like a long dream. Wake up, wake up. Behold the Self which shines like a sun.

416.   You have nothing to do with birth, sorrow, sin and delusion. Abandon all these notions and rest in the Self.

417. The infinite consciousness alone exists, naught else exists.

418. Consciousness does not truly undergo any modification nor does it become impure.

419. Since that omnipresent infinite consciousness alone is present at all times, diversity is absurd and impossible.

420. The reality is beginningless and endless and it is not even reflected in anything: that is the reality.

421. Nothing is created in or by cosmic consciousness for it remains unchanged and unmodified.

422. The mountain seen in a dream only appears to exist in time and space. It does not occupy any space nor does it take time to appear and disappear. Even so is the case with the world.

423. This world-illusion has arisen because of the movement of thought in the mind; when that ceases the illusion will cease, too, and the mind becomes no-mind.

424. The unreal alone dies and it is the unreal that is born again apparently in another body.

425. Wherever the world is seen, that is but an illusory world-appearance. This illusion, and therefore bondage, is sustained by psychological conditioning. Such conditioning is bondage and its abandonment is freedom.

426. Because the "world" is in fact only an appearance, it is in reality emptiness, void and unreal.

427. The world-appearance is illusory.

428. That which is born of the unreal must be unreal, too. Hence, though this world appears to be real, as it is born of the unreal concept, it should be firmly rejected.

429. Just as one who is immersed in the dream sees the dream as utterly real, one who is immersed in this creation thinks that it is utterly real. Just as one goes from one dream to another, one goes from one delusion to another delusion and thus experiences this world as utterly real.

430. It is on account of ignorance that this long-dream world-appearance appears to be real.

431. It is by Self-knowledge that the unreality of the concepts concerning worldly objects is realized.

432. Consciousness does not undergo any change: the only apparent change is the illusory appearance which is illusory and therefore not real!

433. The external phenomena are utterly useless.

434. There is but one consciousness which is pure, invisible, the subtlest of the subtle, tranquil, which is neither the world nor its activities.

435. There is no such thing as creation. You are neither the doer of actions nor the enjoyer of experiences. You are the all, ever at peace, unborn and perfect.

436. The world has no basis at all.

437. It is the movement of thought that appears as this world.

438. This world-appearance is like a dream.

439. On the awakening of the inner intelligence, the world-perception ceases and there arises psychological freedom or non-attachment. That is known as emancipation.

440. There is nothing other than the Self.

441. What appears to be the world is the expansion of one's own notions or thoughts.

442. It is only when the eyes are blinded by ignorance that one perceives the world of diversity.

443. Creation has not taken place. It is but an appearance like the mirage.

444. You are a knower. Whether you know something or do not, remain free from doubt. When you realize that you are the unborn, infinite consciousness, then all ignorance and foolishness cease and this world-appearance ceases.

445. All these worlds, etc. come into being and cease to be as notions and nothing more. Consciousness does not undergo any change in all these. In consciousness there is no experience of pleasure or pain, nor does a notion arise in it as "This I am."

446. There is the unreal experience of this world and what is known as the other-world, though all these are false.

447. He who does not abandon his confirmed conviction in the existence of diversity is not abandoned by sorrow.

448. When one falls into this illusion of world-appearance, he is at once preyed upon by countless other illusions which arise in the original illusion.

449. If you close your eyes, the vision of the external world is blotted out: if you remove the notion of the world from your consciousness, pure consciousness alone exists.

450. The world and the "I" exist only as notions, not as fact nor as reality.

451. Creation, world, movement of consciousness, etc. are mere words without substance. When such ideas are abandoned, the "world" and the "I" cease to be and consciousness alone exists, pure and immutable. This unconditioned consciousness alone is, naught else is – not even the nature of diverse objects here.

452. The illusory appearance of objects is of no practical use.

453. When you affirm the reality of the illusory appearance, you invite unhappiness; when its unreality is realized there is great happiness.

454. The notion of the reality of the objects of this world arises only in ignorance.

455. Confusion or delusion is unreal and the unreal does not exist.

456. In their mind, my body seems to be real; but to my illumined intelligence, their physical existence is unreal, as it is to a sleeping person.

457. When one is fully established in the Self, then this world-appearance ceases like dream during deep sleep.

458. As surely as it is a certainty that where there is sunlight there is illumination, where there is experience of the essencelessness of the worldly objects, there occurs spiritual awakening.

459. The world-appearance arises in ignorance and wisdom puts an end to it.

460.   When what exists is realized as it is, the world-appearance ceases.

461.   Do not be deluded by this illusory world-appearance.

462.   To the man of Self-knowledge what the ignorant man thinks real (time, space, matter, etc.) are non-existent.

463.   In the eyes of the wise man there is no world.

464.   That is known as the attainment of the highest in which one abandons the notions of the existence of objects and in which one rests in one's own pure Self. When all divisions are given up, the indivisible alone remains. It is pure, one, beginningless and endless.

465.   When wisdom is strengthened and confirmed, and when the impurity of conditioning is washed away, the holy one shines with an extraordinary radiance. Both the inner notion and the external perception of the world cease for him.

466.   Behold the entire universe composed of you, I, mountains, gods and demons, etc. as you would behold the creations and the happenings of a dream.

467.   I saw many universes and their diversity aroused my curiosity. I wanted to roam more and more to see the magnitude of creation. After some time, I abandoned that idea knowing that it was delusion and remained established in the infinite consciousness. Instantly, all this perception of diversity vanished from my sight. There was the pure consciousness, nothing else. This is the truth: all else is imagination, notion, delusion or illusory perception.

468.   There is no such thing as earth or matter.

469.   Duality or diversity is false: the one mass of infinite consciousness alone is real.

470.   There is no such thing as the world.

471.   This body is but pure void, it seems to exist on account of the mental conditioning. When the latter ceases, the body ceases to be seen or experienced, just as the dream-object is not experienced on waking up.

472.   Neither the subtle body nor the gross body is seen even in the waking state when the mental conditioning ceases.

473.   This universe has no form, no body, no materiality, though it seems to have a form.

474.   You imagine that I have a body. It is on account of this notion existing in you that I produce this sound known as speech. You hear it even as a sleeping person hears sounds in his dream.

475. The diversity perceived in a dream does not create a diversity in the dreamer; even so the notion of a creation does not create a division in consciousness. Consciousness alone is, no creation; the dream-mountain is the dreamer, not a mountain.

476. The world is an appearance and not existence.

477. What is unreal is unreal, even if it has been experienced for a long time by all.

478. Neither in the waking state or in dream is there a real world.

479. When sleep has ceased, the world-appearance rises; when that ceases there is pure consciousness. That "nothing" which remains after everything has been negated as "not this, not this" is pure consciousness.

480. In the vision of the knowers of the truth, there is nothing other than the pure and infinite consciousness, and the objective universe is completely and totally non-existent.

481. Besides this there are other universes of which I have not told you. For of what use is investigation into the nature of the world and others which are but of the nature of a dream; wise men do not waste their time talking about useless things.

482. When Self-knowledge arises, the illusory notion of a world-existence vanishes.

483. Though the body-notion is unreal it is experienced as if it were real, just like the dream-object.

484. Even the original creation is like a dream. It is but an illusory appearance. Though devoid of earth, and all the rest of it, it appears to have earth, etc.

485. The original dreamlike creation of the world and also the dream that we experience now are both unreal.

486. There is no death, and by the same token there is no birth either.

487. Realize that this world-appearance with all its contradictions is nothing more than appearance which is non-existent.

488. That which is firmly believed to exist is experienced by that person physically, for the body is only mind.

489. Just as some people remember their dreams, some people also remember their past existences.

490. Consciousness is infinite peace which exists forever unmodified.

491. It is good to remind yourself that all this is but a long dream.

492. Just as the dream-mountain is realized as pure void when the dreamer wakes up, even so are all these forms realized to be non-existent when one is enlightened.

493.   When the wise one realizes that this world is like a dream-city, his hopes are not centered in it.

494.   Only when it is realized that there is no creation at all does real Self-knowledge arise which leads to liberation.   Such liberation is unending, infinite and unconditioned.

495.   The objective universe is delusion or illusion; it does not disappear except through persistent practice.

496.   Whatever objects are perceived in this world are the mind only, even as the dream-objects are the mind only.

497.   In this subtle body there arise the thoughts or concepts of physical bodies and their component parts, concepts of birth, activity, etc., concepts of time, space, sequence, etc., as also concepts of old age, death, virtue and defect, knowledge, etc. Having conjured up these concepts, the subtle body itself experiences the objective universe composed of the five elements as if it existed in reality. But all this is surely illusory, like dream-objects and dream-experiences.

498.   When there is the notion of reality in unreal phenomena, there is bondage.

499.   Something which is unreal does not arise in the real.

500.   There is no illusion in the infinite.

501.   This illusion of world-appearance vanishes when one is awakened and enlightened.   Then one realizes that it has never been, it is not and it will never be.

502.   The unreal does not exist at all at any time.

503.   When dream is realized as dream, the false notion vanishes.   Awareness drops its object and rests in the infinite consciousness.

504.   This world has arisen like a dream.

505.   Nothing, not even this body, has ever been created.

506.   Like a frog in the blind well, foolish and ignorant people base their understanding on the experience of the moment and, on account of their perverse understanding, they are deluded into thinking that the body alone is the source of experience or awareness.

507.   What you have called the body does not exist in the eyes of the sage.

508.   There is no "dream" in the infinite consciousness. There is neither a body nor a dream in it.

509.   Though this universe seems to have existed for a long time and though it seems to be a functional reality, still it is pure void and it is no more real than an imaginary city.

510. Nothing exists here and therefore there are no concepts of objects; there is nothing other than the Self and the Self does not conceive of an object.

511. It is only as long as you are not fully enlightened that you experience apparent diversity.

SRI SANKARA
(512 – 524)

512. Where has the world gone? Who has removed it, or where has it disappeared to? I saw it only just now, and now it is not there.

513. The products of natural causation, from the idea of doership down to the body itself and all its senses, are also unreal in view of the way they are changing every moment, while one's true nature itself never changes.

514. Give up identification with this mass of flesh as well as with what thinks it a mass. Both are intellectual imaginations. Recognize your true Self as undifferentiated awareness, unaffected by time, past, present or future, and enter Peace.

515.   The living organism, which is thought to belong to oneself through its identification with the intellect, does not really exist. On the other hand, the true Self is quite distinct from it, and the identification of oneself with the intellect is due to misunderstanding.

516.   The mistaken imagination of illusion is not a reality.

517.   As the darkness, that is its opposite, is melted away in the radiance of the sun, so, indeed, all things visible are melted away in the Eternal.

518.   Reaching bodiless purity, mere Being, partless, the being of the Eternal, the sage returns to this world no more.

519.   I see not, nor hear, nor know aught of this world; for I bear the mark of the Self, whose form is being and bliss.

520.   The belief in this world is built up of unreality.

521.   The world no longer is, whether past, present, or to come, after awakening to the supreme reality, in the real Self, the Eternal, from all wavering free.

522.   All changing forms in nature beginning with personality and ending with the body, and all sensual objects; these are unreal, because subject to change every moment; but the Self never changes.

523.   There is no freedom for him who is full of attachment to the body and its like; for him who is free, there is no wish for the body and its like; the dreamer is not awake, he who is awake dreams not; for these things are the opposites of each other.

524.   In as much as all this world, body and organs, vital breath and personality are all unreal, in so much THOU ART THAT, the restful, the stainless, secondless Eternal, the supreme.

STEP THREE

See how the impostor self perpetuates its imaginary self and all illusion and suffering.

SRI RAMANA MAHARSHI
(525 – 545)

525. So long as one retains a trace of individuality, one is a seeker still, and not a true seer effort free, even though one's penance and one's powers may be wonderful indeed.

526. Poor fellow, you who are so proud of your omniscience, when you are questioned, "You who know all things, do you know who you are?" you collapse disgraced, discomfited. O man of genius, may this your ego-mind dry up as dust and perish utterly.

527. Unless by one means or another mind dies out and certitude from true Self-recognition comes, the knowledge which mere learning brings is like the horse's horn unreal.

528. When ego ends, then one becomes a devotee true; when ego ends, one becomes a knower too; when ego ends one becomes Being supreme. When ego ends, grace fills all space.

529.   Since every vice springs from the false pleasures of swerving from the Self, the plentitude of virtue is the perfect peace of pure awareness following the end of the ego which is by such false pleasures fed.

530.   When ego goes, there is no loss of Being. Hence be not afraid.

531.   The separate ego wholly dead, the indivisible Self as pure awareness brightly shines. This I is not the false conceptual self earth-bound and body-bound.

532.   When the ego-life dissolves and dies in silence, then one lives the life supreme of pure awareness. When the false ego dream-like fades into its source, the true Self rises of its own accord.

533.   Great knowers recognize no other bondage than the rising movements of the mind and they find true release nowhere but in the total death, leaving no trace behind, of every movement of the mind.

534.   The false dream ends when we wake up. Even so, the ego dies when the sun, the true I, rises. Ego's destruction by strong Self-inquiry is what is known as Self-attainment.

535.   Only for those free from all sense of doership the bliss of tranquil peace shines pure within. For the ego proud is the sole evil seed whence spring all known calamities.

536.   Whether one is or one is not engaged in work, one gains the state of non-action only when the ego with its proud delusion "I am the doer" has died and disappeared.

537.   The bright Awareness, our true Being, is the sole Truth the Heart should cherish. The triads we perceive should be despised and driven away as dreams created by the treacherous mind.

538.   Beside the Self nothing in truth exists. But then the deep delusion that the body is oneself makes one let go the solid, non-dual bliss of immortality and fall into birth and death.

539.   Of all the demonic qualities the basis is the ego.

540.   Those who have made the hardest sacrifice, that of the ego, have nothing more to renounce.

541.   Losing the false ego in awareness, and firm abidance as awareness is true clarity.

542.   Unlike the ego which rises and sets, the true Self abides for ever the same. Turn your back on the false ego, and so destroy it, and then shine as the one Self alone.

543.   Even as the ego does not die unless the Self's glance falls on it, the painful dream of this phenomenal world will never disappear unless the mind meets glorious death.

544.   The true light of Awareness pure, subtle, egoless, non-objective, silent, which tires the mind and baffles it till it admits "I know not", this is Being-Awareness, this the Self.

545.   Here in this earthly life there is no greater good than gaining the grandeur of the Self supreme. To gain it and enjoy it, search within and first destroy the ego false and worthless.

SRI MURUGANAR
(546 – 559)

546.   The nature of my realization was such that the 'I' that asserts its own reality was revealed as false and disappeared, but not the 'I' that is the unique, pure, non-dual Self that exists permeating all things equally.

547.   In the heart the absolute purity of imperishable grace wells up as consciousness, the supreme, so that the false deceitful mind that says 'I' is destroyed and disappears, no longer having any duality whatsoever to dwell upon. I exist in the heart, with the heart itself as my real nature.

548.   In the hearts of true devotees that are infused with the noble light of grace, the dark ignorance of the ghostly ego, unable to operate, will disappear. In the mind in which the delusive and destructive ego has completely died the glory of grace will spontaneously shine forth in abundance.

549.   Other than being-consciousness there is no reliable support whatsoever for the soul. Grace itself is nothing less than this same being-consciousness. When the impetuous warring ego, which feeds on the mind's deceit, finally subsides in the heart, it is that same being-consciousness that manifests as the life of flooding grace.

550.   Until we eliminate the ghost-like ego – the infatuation that arises through lack of Self-attention – the unified consciousness of the Real will not arise. Similarly, until that unified consciousness of the Real arises, the true love that is free of duality will not rise up in the heart.

551.   As long as we do not free ourselves from the state of inattention in which the unified state of the Self – that exists as pure consciousness – is subverted through the ego, the state of love that is the fullness of the Real, free of all differentiation, will not be experienced in the heart.

552. The enlightened state, in which the grace and wisdom of the Self is directly experienced, will not come into being unless we separate ourselves from the illusory world of the divided mind so that it can no longer exist. Therefore we must thoroughly investigate and comprehend our own Self, so that the hostility of the ghost-like ego, that brings with it the torment of an understanding based on differentiation, may cease.

553. Through tenacious inquiry into the Self the pure 'I' springs forth, eliminating the false personal identity. We should realize that that true 'I', filled with the light of our own true nature, is the supreme reality itself.

554. Dualistic concepts such as 'I' and 'He' are a treacherous trick of the mind that assumes the form of the body. Eliminate therefore this powerful mental imagination and discern the Self.

555. Even now, if you entirely eradicate the personal ego based on the multifarious nature of the non-Self, you will experience an intense and limitless awakening, as your true nature, the supreme Self, shines out.

556. Realization in all its clarity flourished in the form of Self-consciousness, the light of Truth shining in the Heart as the vast expanse in which there is no arising of the contemptible ego.

557. The death of the ego, which arises as 'I' in conjunction with the body's physical form, is synonymous with a new existence in the luminous firmament of the supreme, free of the embodied mind's forgetfulness of the Self.

558. The ego self is like a poison which has its origin in and thrives upon a fundamental misapprehension. Here in the world it is an enemy masquerading as a friend and you should root up and cast out every last vestige of it.

559. Allow reality to shine as it truly is without any obstacle whatsoever by means of the destruction of the age-old deceit of the hostile ego.

SRI ANNAMALAI SWAMI
(560 – 564)

560. The substratum upon which the false idea of the mind has been superimposed is the Self. When you see the mind, the Self, the underlying substratum, is not seen. It is hidden by a false but persistent idea. And, conversely, when the Self is seen there is no mind.

561.   Realizing the Self is the only useful and worthy activity in this life, so keep the body in good repair till that goal is achieved. Afterwards, the Self will take care of everything and you won't have to worry about anything any more. In fact, you won't be able to, because the mind that previously did the worrying, the choosing and the discriminating will no longer be there. In that state you won't need it and you won't miss it.

562.   Questioner: So, you are saying that believing that I am a body and a particular person is purely imagination. Or better still, a bad habit that I should try to go get rid of?

Annamalai Swami: Correct. This habit has become very strong because you have reinforced and strengthened it over many lifetimes. This will go if you meditate on your real Self. The habit will melt away, like ice becoming water.

563.   The mind only gets dissolved in the Self by constant practice. At that moment the 'I am the body' idea disappears, just as darkness disappears when the sun rises.

564.   The body is not the Self; the mind is not the Self. The real 'I' is the Self, and nothing ever happens to or affects the Self.

565.   The happiness obtained through the second kind of absorption, the destruction of the mind, is eternal. It is the supreme bliss.

566.   Temporary quiescence of the mind is temporary quiescence of misery, and permanent destruction of the mind is permanent destruction of misery; that is, the mind itself is misery! Hence let us find out what is to be done to destroy the mind.

567.   When Self, our nature of existence-consciousness, instead of shining only as the pure consciousness 'I am', shines mixed with an adjunct as 'I am a man, I am Rama, I am so-and-so, I am this or that', then this mixed consciousness is the ego. This mixed consciousness can rise only by catching hold of a name and form. When we feel 'I am a man, I am Rama, I am sitting, I am lying', is it not clear that we have mistaken the body for 'I', and that we have assumed its name and postures as 'I am this and I am thus'?

SRI NISARGADATTA MAHARAJ
(568 – 628)

568.   As to my mind, there is no such thing.

569.   When you believe yourself to be a person, you see persons everywhere. In reality there are no persons, only threads of memories and habits. At the moment of realization the person ceases. Identity remains, but identity is not a person, it is inherent in the reality itself.

570.   Of what use is the relative view to you? You are able to look from the absolute point of view – why go back to the relative? Are you afraid of the absolute?

571.   Questioner: I am engaged in the study of philosophy, sociology and education. I think more mental development is needed before I can dream of Self-realization. Am I on the right track?

Maharaj: To earn a livelihood some specialized knowledge is needed. General knowledge develops the mind, no doubt. But if you are going to spend your life in amassing knowledge, you build a wall round yourself. To go beyond the mind, a well-furnished mind is not needed.

Questioner: Then what is needed?

Maharaj: Distrust your mind, and go beyond.

Questioner: What shall I find beyond the mind?

Maharaj: The direct experience of being, knowing and loving.

572.   I take my stand where no difference exists, where things are not, nor the minds that create them. There I am at home.

573.   As long as you do not see that it is mere habit, built on memory, prompted by desire, you will think yourself to be a person – living, feeling, thinking, active, passive, pleased or pained.   Question yourself, ask yourself, 'Is it so?' 'Who am I?' 'What is behind and beyond all this?'   And soon you will see your mistake.

574.   There are so many who take the dawn for the noon, a momentary experience for full realization and destroy even the little they gain by excess of pride.

575.   The sun of truth remains hidden behind the cloud of self-identification with the body.

576.   The realized man is egoless; he has lost the capacity of identifying himself with anything.   He is without location, placeless, beyond space and time, beyond the world.   Beyond words and thoughts is he.

577.   The false self must be abandoned before the real Self can be found.

578.   Resolutely remind yourself that you are not the mind and that its problems are not yours.

579.   That immovable state, which is not affected by the birth and death of a body or a mind, that state you must perceive.

580. Have your being outside of this body of birth and death and all your problems will be solved. They exist because you believe yourself born to die. Undeceive yourself and be free. You are not a person.

581. You have to be very alert, or else your mind will play false with you. It is like watching a thief – not that you expect anything from a thief, but you do not want to be robbed.

582. Your personality dissolves and only the witness remains.

583. Any name or shape you give yourself obscures your real nature.

584. All your problems arise because you have defined and therefore limited yourself. When you do not think yourself to be this or that, all conflict ceases.

585. There is no such thing as a person.

586. Don't ask the mind to confirm what is beyond the mind. Direct experience is the only valid confirmation.

587. Without Self-realization, no virtue is genuine.

588. By looking tirelessly, I became quite empty and with that emptiness all came back to me except the mind.

589. Beyond the mind all distinctions cease.

590.   Questioner: How does one shape one's character?

Maharaj: By seeing it as it is, and being sincerely sorry. This integral seeing-feeling can work miracles.

591.   The higher can be had only through freedom from the lower.

592.   Insanity is universal. Sanity is rare. Yet there is hope, because the moment we perceive our insanity, we are on the way to sanity.

593.   Questioner: Yet we are afraid of the better and cling to the worse.

Maharaj: This is our stupidity, verging on insanity.

594.   The false self wants to continue – pleasantly.

595.   The only radical solution is to dissolve the separate sense of 'I am such-and-such person' once and for good.

596.   The mind is a cheat.

597.   I know myself as I am in reality. I am neither the body, nor the mind, nor the mental faculties. I am beyond all these.

598.   It is the 'I am the body' idea that is so calamitous. It blinds you completely to your real nature. Even for a moment do not think that you are the body.

599.   Maharaj: When the mind is kept away from its preoccupations, it becomes quiet. If you do not disturb this quiet and stay in it, you find that it is permeated with a light and a love you have never known; and yet you recognize it at once as your own nature. Once you have passed through this experience, you will never be the same man again; the unruly mind may break its peace and obliterate its vision; but it is bound to return, provided the effort is sustained; until the day when all bonds are broken, delusions and attachments end and life becomes supremely concentrated in the present.

Questioner: What difference does it make?

Maharaj: The mind is no more. There is only love in action.

600.   Trace every action to its selfish motive and look at the motive intently till it dissolves.

601.   Even the idea of being man or woman, or even human, should be discarded.

602.   The person you became at birth and will cease to be at death is temporary and false. You are not the sensual, emotional and intellectual person, gripped by desires and fears. Find out your real being.

603.   It is the mind that tells you that the mind is there. Don't be deceived. All the endless arguments about the mind are produced by the mind itself, for its own protection, continuation and expansion. It is the blank refusal to consider the convolutions and convulsions of the mind that can take you beyond it.

604. Keep on remembering: I am neither the mind nor its ideas. Do it patiently and with conviction and you will surely come to the direct vision of yourself as the source of being – knowing – loving, eternal, all-embracing, all-pervading. You are the infinite focused in a body. Now you see the body only. Try earnestly and you will come to see the infinite only.

605. You have never been, nor shall ever be a person. Refuse to consider yourself as one.

606. The person is merely the result of a misunderstanding. In reality, there is no such thing. Feelings, thoughts and actions race before the watcher in endless succession, leaving traces in the brain and creating an illusion of continuity. A reflection of the watcher in the mind creates the sense of 'I' and the person acquires an apparently independent existence. In reality there is no person, only the watcher identifying himself with the 'I' and the 'mine.'

607. The sense of identity will remain, but no longer identification with a particular body. Being – awareness – love will shine in full splendor. Liberation is never of the person, it is always from the person.

608. The person is but a shell imprisoning you. Break the shell.

609. The reward of Self-knowledge is freedom from the personal self.

610.　The death of the mind is the birth of wisdom.

611.　I am not the mind, never was, nor shall be.

612.　When you know that you are neither body nor mind, you will not be swayed by them.

613.　The dissolution of personality is followed always by a sense of great relief, as if a heavy burden has fallen off.

614.　It is not you who desires, fears and suffers, it is the person built on the foundation of your body by circumstances and influences. You are not that person.

615.　To know that you are a prisoner of your mind, that you live in an imaginary world of your own creation, is the dawn of wisdom. To want nothing of it, to be ready to abandon it entirely, is earnestness.

616.　You must be free from the person you take yourself to be, for it is the idea you have of yourself that keeps you in bondage.

617.　Get busy with your ego – leave me alone. As long as you are locked up within your mind, my state is beyond your grasp.

618.　At present you are moved by the pleasure-pain principle which is the ego.

619. The ego, like a crooked mirror, narrows down and distorts. It is the worst of all the tyrants, it dominates you absolutely.

620. Freedom from the ego-self is the fruit of Self-inquiry.

621. To be a person is to be asleep.

622. What prevents you from knowing yourself as all and beyond all is the mind based on memory. It has power over you as long as you trust it; don't struggle with it; just disregard it. Deprived of attention, it will slow down and reveal the mechanism of its working. Once you know its nature and purpose, you will not allow it to create imaginary problems.

623. Only when you know yourself as entirely alien to and different from the body, will you find respite from the mixture of fear and craving inseparable from 'I-am-the-body' idea.

624. When the mind is quiet it reflects reality. When it is motionless through and through, it dissolves and only reality remains. This reality is so concrete, so actual, so much more tangible than mind and matter, that compared to it even diamond is soft like butter. This overwhelming actuality makes the world dreamlike, misty, irrelevant.

625. With the dissolution of the personal 'I', personal suffering disappears.

626. It is only your mind that prevents Self-knowledge.

627. Rebel against your slavery to your mind, see your bonds as self-created and break the chains of attachment and revulsion.

628. To be what you are, you must go beyond the mind, into your own being. It is immaterial what is the mind that you leave behind, provided you leave it behind for good. This again is not possible without Self-realization.

THE SUPREME YOGA
(629 – 768)

629. Spreading the net of worldly objects of pleasure, it is this egotism that traps the living beings. Indeed, all the terrible calamities in this world are born of egotism. Egotism eclipses self-control, destroys virtue, and dissipates equanimity.

630. It is this mind alone which is the cause of all objects of the world; the three worlds exist because of the mind-stuff; when the mind vanishes, the worlds vanish too.

631. One's own mind has become one's worst enemy. Egotism is the foremost cause for evil.

632. This diversity arises on account of mental modifications and it will cease when they cease.

633. As long as one clings to the notion of the reality of "you" and "I", there is no liberation. Not by merely verbally denying such a notion of existence is it obliterated.

634. Thought is mind; there is no distinction between the two.

635. When the mind disintegrates, there is liberation, and there is no more rebirth; for it was mind alone that appeared to take birth and to die.

636. Only a fool, not a wise man, is deluded by his own ideas; it is a fool who thinks that the imperishable is perishable and gets deluded. Egotism is but an idea, based on a false association of the Self with the physical elements.

637. Egotism promotes cravings; without it they perish.

638.   Abandon your reliance on fate or gods created by dull-witted people and by self-effort and Self-knowledge make the mind no-mind.

639.   When the mind is absorbed in the infinite consciousness there is supreme peace; but when the mind is involved in thoughts there is great sorrow. The restlessness of the mind itself is known as ignorance or nescience; it is the seat of tendencies, predispositions or conditioning – destroy this through inquiry, as also by the firm abandonment of contemplation of objects of sense-pleasure.

640.   "I", "mine" etc. have no existence at all; the one Self alone is the truth at all times.

641.   Do not get tangled with the moods of your mind, but be established in truth. Regard the mind as a foreigner or a piece of wood or stone. There is no mind in infinite consciousness; that which is done by this non-existent mind is also unreal. Be established in this realization.

642.   That the mind is impure is the experience of everyone who strives for liberation.

643.   Be established in truth and live in freedom in a mindless state.

644. The notions of "I" and "mine" are the eager receptacles which receive sorrow and suffering. He who identifies the body with the Self sinks in misery.

645. Worldliness sprouts from the seed of the ego-sense.

646. Abandon this ego-sense with all the strength that lies within.

647. The one infinite consciousness, which is of the nature of pure bliss, is eclipsed by the shadow of the ego-sense.

648. All these notions of 'I' and 'you' are unreal.

649. The practice of restraint bestows great joy and auspiciousness upon you. Hence, resort to self-restraint, give up ego-sense.

650. Only the supreme truth exists and the individual personality is absorbed in it.

651. This notion of the "I" cannot be got rid of except through Self-knowledge.

652. Pursuing the inquiry into its real nature, the mind abandons its identification even with the body.

653. When the mind gets involved in the external objective universe, it moves away from the Self.

654. The mind is naught but ideas and notions.

655.   Reality is veiled by the mind and revealed when the mind ceases.

656.   In this world the cause of all misfortunes is only the mind which is full of sorrow and grief, desire and delusion.   Forgetful of Self-knowledge, it generates desire and anger, evil thoughts and cravings which throw the person into the fire of sense-objects.

657.   When even the notion of the ego-sense has ceased, you will be like the infinite space.

658.   When the limited and conditioned feeling "I am so-and-so" ceases, there arises consciousness of the all-pervading infinite.   Hence, you too abandon the false and fanciful notion of the ego-sense within your own heart.   When this ego-sense is dispelled, the supreme light of Self-knowledge will surely shine in your heart. This ego-sense alone is the densest form of darkness: when it is dispelled, the inner light shines by itself.

659.   In truth, there is no mind.

660.   When the inner light begins to shine, the mind ceases to be, even as when there is light, darkness vanishes.

661.   Be firmly established in egolessness and remain unpolluted like space.

662.   The mind is the hub around which this vicious cycle revolves, creating delusion in the minds of the deluded. It is by firmly restraining that hub through intense self-effort and keen intelligence, that the whole wheel is brought to a standstill. When the hub's motion is stopped the wheel does not revolve: when the mind is stilled, illusion ceases. One who does not know this trick and does not practice it, undergoes endless sorrow.

663.   You will also enjoy freedom when the mind ceases to be, along with the world-illusion contained in it.

664.   Consciousness free from the limitations of the mind is known as the inner intelligence: it is the essential nature of no-mind, and therefore it is not tainted by the impurities of concepts and percepts. That is the reality, that is supreme auspiciousness, that is the state known as the supreme Self, that is omniscience, and that vision is not had when the wicked mind functions.

665.   Be without the mind and realize that you are pure consciousness.

666.   Mind is like a tree which is firmly rooted in the vicious field known as body. Worries and anxieties are its blossoms; it is laden with the fruits of old age and disease; it is adorned with the flowers of desires and sense-enjoyments; hopes and longings are its branches; and perversities are its leaves.

667.　Mind is like a crow which dwells in the nest of this body.　It revels in filth; it waxes strong by consuming flesh; it pierces the hearts of others; it knows only its own point of view which it considers as the truth; it is dark on account of its ever-growing stupidity; it is full of evil tendencies; and it indulges in violent expressions.　It is a burden on earth; drive it far, far away from yourself.

668.　Mind is like a monkey.　It roams from one place to another, seeking fruits (rewards, pleasures, etc.); bound to this world-cycle it dances and entertains people.　Restrain it from all sides if you wish to attain perfection.

669.　Tranquillize the mind with the help of the mind itself.　For ever abandon every form of mental agitation. Remain at peace within yourself like a tree freed from the disturbance caused by monkeys.

670.　I am that which is indivisible, which has no name nor change, which is beyond all concepts of unity and diversity, which is beyond measure and other than which naught else is.　Hence, O mind, I abandon you who are the source of sorrow.

671.　Alas, for so long I have been victimized by ignorance:　but, luckily, I have discovered that which robbed me of Self-knowledge!　I shall never more be the victim of ignorance.

672.　In the absence of Self-knowledge, there arose ego-sense:　but now, I am free of ego-sense.

673.   After having abandoned the very root of the ego-sense, I rest in the Self which is of the nature of peace.

674.   The ego-sense is the source of endless sorrow, suffering and evil action.

675.   If the ego-sense ceases to be, then the illusory world-appearance does not germinate again and all cravings come to an end.

676.   It is only a fool that entertains a feeling "This I am" in relation to that temporary appearance known as the body etc.

677.   It is my fault that I still cling to the notion that you, my mind, is a real entity. When I realize that all these phenomena are illusory appearances, then you will become no-mind and all the memories of sense-experiences, etc. will come to an end.

678.   It is by the destruction of the mind that there can be happiness.

679.   Mind is like a forest with thought-forms for its trees and cravings for its creepers: by destroying these, I attain bliss.

680.   Where there is Self-knowledge, there is neither mind nor the senses, nor the tendencies and habits (the concepts and percepts). I have attained that supreme state. I have emerged victorious. I have attained liberation.

681.   Since all delusion has come to an end, since the mind has ceased to be and all evil thoughts have vanished, I rest peacefully in my own Self.

682.   When the mind has ceased to be because of the total absence of the notions of material existence, consciousness exists in its own nature as consciousness: and that is known as pure being. When consciousness devoid of notions of objectivity merges in itself losing its separate identity as it were, it is pure being. When all objects, external (material) and internal (notional) merge in consciousness, there is pure being of consciousness. This is the supreme vision which happens to all liberated ones, whether they seem to have a body or they are without one. This vision is available to one who has been "awakened", to one who is in a state of deep contemplation, and to a man of Self-knowledge; it is not experienced by the ignorant person.

683.   There is no such thing as "I" nor "the world." There is no mind, nor an object of knowledge, nor the world-illusion.

684.   I am not the enjoyments, nor do they belong to me; this intellect and the sense-organs are not me, nor are they mine – they are inert and I am sentient. I am not the mind which is the root-cause of this ignorant cycle of birth and death.

685.   The nature of enlightenment is known only by direct experience.

686.   So long as one does not subdue the mind with the mind, one cannot attain Self-knowledge; and as long as one entertains the false notions of "I" and "mine", so long sorrow does not come to an end.

687.   In the twinkling of an eye, this little ripple known as the mind assumes terrible proportions. Man foolishly ascribes to the Self the sorrow and the sufferings that do not touch it in the least and becomes miserable.

688.   All these that constitute the world-illusion come into being like a mirage in the desert. This illusion spreads out like waves in the ocean, assuming various names like mind, the faculty of discrimination, the ego-sense, the latent tendencies and the senses. The mind and the ego-sense are not in fact two but one and the same: the distinction is verbal. The mind is the ego-sense and what is known as the ego-sense is the mind.

689.   Bring about the cessation of the mind.

690.   Mind and movement of thought are inseparable; and the cessation of one is the cessation of both.

691.   Mind should be destroyed.

692.   You do not exist, O mind.

693.   For a very long time, this ghost of a mind generated countless evil notions like lust, anger, etc. Now that that ghost has been laid, I laugh at my own past foolishness. The mind is dead; all my worries and anxieties are dead; the demon known as ego-sense is dead.

694. When the mind ceases to be, the craving ceases to be too. When the mind is dead and the craving is dead, delusion has vanished and egolessness is born. Hence, I am awakened in this state of wakefulness.

695. Thoughts are utterly useless, now that the mind is dead.

696. O mind, when you cease to be, all the good and noble qualities blossom. There is peace and purity of heart. People do not fall into doubt and error. There is friendship which promotes the happiness of all. Worries and anxieties dry up. When the darkness of ignorance is dispelled, the inner light shines brightly. Mental distraction and distress cease, just as when the wind ceases to agitate its surface, the ocean becomes calm. There arises Self-knowledge within and the realization of truth puts an end to the perception of the world-illusion: the infinite consciousness alone shines. There is an experience of bliss.

697. The existence of the mind causes misery; and its cessation brings joy.

698. As long there is mind, there is no cessation of sorrow. When the mind ceases, the world-appearance also ceases to be. The mind is the seed for misery.

699. The very nature of the mind is stupidity.

700. It is not possible to "kill the mind" without proper methods.

701. Be free of the ego-sense and rejoice in the Self.

702.   As long as the concepts born of ignorance persist, as long as there is perception of that which is not the infinite and as long as there is hope in the trap known as the world, so long one entertains notions of mind, etc. As long as one considers the body as the "I" and as long as the Self is related to what is seen, as long as there is hope in objects with the feeling "this is mine", so long there will be delusion concerning mind, etc.

703.   When incorrect perception has come to an end and when the sun of Self-knowledge arises in the heart, know that the mind is reduced to naught. It is not seen again.

704.   The mental conditioning has vanished. The mind has come to an end.

705.   The Self is not affected by the body, nor is the body in any way related to the Self.

706.   The individual is nothing more than the personalized mind. Individuality ceases when that mind ceases.

707.   This ignorance has become dense by having been expressed and experienced in thousands of incarnations, within and outside this body by the senses. But, Self-knowledge is not within the reach of the senses. It arises when the senses and the mind, which is the sixth sense, cease.

708.   Give up this subservience to the ghost known as ego-sense and rest in the Self.

709.   You are the Self, not the mind.

710.   The goblin-mind residing in the body has nothing to do with the Self, yet it quietly assumes "I am the self." This is the cause of birth and death. This assumption robs you of courage.

711.   If it is realized that the perceived mind itself is unreal, then it is clear that the perceived world is unreal too.

712.   The mind of the knower of the truth is no-mind.

713.   He who is polluted by the ego-sense, whether he is a learned scholar or one superior even to that, he indeed is a wicked man.

714.   This creation is no doubt born of ignorance and the belief in creation destroys true perception. Though this creation is unreal, yet on account of the emergence of the ego-sense, it appears to be solidly real.

715.   The cause of this world-appearance and bondage is indeed the mind.

716.   The best method is by inquiring into the nature of the Self which is infinite. Your mind will be completely absorbed. Then both the mind and the inquiry will cease. Remain firmly established in what remains after that.

717. This supreme consciousness alone exists. It is the supreme truth, untainted by any impurity, for ever in a state of perfect equilibrium and devoid of ego-sense. Once this truth is realized, it shines constantly without setting.

718. I am pure consciousness, devoid of ego-sense and all-pervading. There is neither birth nor death for this consciousness.

719. One thing still remains to be renounced: your ego-sense. If the heart abandons the mind, there is realization of the absolute.

720. Worries (or movements of thought) alone are known as mind. Thought (notion, concept) is another name for the same thing.

721. The utter destruction or extinction of the mind is the extinction of the creation-cycle. It is also known as the abandonment of the mind. Therefore, uproot this tree whose seed is the "I"-idea, with all its branches, fruits and leaves, and rest in the space in the heart.

722. Realize "I am not that ego-sense" and rest in pure awareness.

723. All notions cease. The falsity which arose as the mind ceases when notions cease.

724. Ignorance lasts only so long as the mind functions.

725. There is no mind in the liberated ones.

726. Renunciation of the mind is total renunciation.

727. The ego-sense is unreal. Do not trust it.

728. The ego-sense looks upon space around it as itself and its possession. Thus it identifies itself with the body, etc. which it desires to protect. The body, etc. exist and perish after some time. On account of this delusion, the ego-sense grieves repeatedly, thinking that the self is dead and lost. When the pot, etc. are lost, the space remains unaffected. Even so, when the bodies are lost, the Self remains unaffected. The Self is pure consciousness, subtler than even space. It is never destroyed. It is unborn. It does not perish.

729. Remain in the pure, egoless state.

730. The notion "I am the body" is bondage; the seeker should avoid it. "I am no-thing but pure consciousness" – such understanding when it is sustained is conducive to liberation. It is only when one does not realize the Self which is free from old age, death, etc. that one wails aloud, "Alas, I am dead or I am helpless." It is by such thoughts that ignorance is fortified. Free your mind from such impure thoughts and notions. Rest in the Self free from such notions.

731. When the ego-sense dies, ignorance perishes and that is known as liberation.

732. All these notions exist in the mind. Subdue the mind by the mind. Purify the mind by the mind. Destroy the mind by the mind.

733.   When the movement of the mind has ceased, the Self shines by its own light. In that light all sorrow comes to an end and there is the bliss which the Self experiences in itself.

734.   I am THAT which is beyond the body, mind and senses.

735.   The abandonment of notions is the supreme good.

736.   The non-perception of objects and the non-arising of notions. This should be experienced.

737.   When the mind abandons its conditioning, the objects lose their temptation.

738.   One who has not abandoned the ego-sense and mine-ness knows neither renunciation nor wisdom nor peace.

739.   The supreme Self is in the supreme Self, the infinite in the infinite, the peace in peace. That is all there is, neither "I" nor "the world" nor "the mind."

740.   When the seed for the world-appearance (which is the ego-sense) has been destroyed, the world-appearance goes with it. Even as the mirror gets misted by moisture, the Self is veiled by the unreal ego-sense. This ego-sense gives rise to all the rest of this world-appearance. When it goes, then the Self shines by its own light, even as the sun shines when the veiling cloud is blown away.

741.   Just as an object thrown into the ocean dissolves in the ocean, the ego-sense which enters the Self is dissolved in it.

742.   Self-knowledge is the realization of the unreality of the ego-sense. Nothing else can ensure your true welfare. Hence, first abandon the individualized ego-sense.

743.   Know that all that you experience in the name of mind, ego-sense, intellect, etc. is nothing but ignorance. This ignorance vanishes through self-effort.

744.   Wherever the ego-sense arises there the world manifests itself. The ego-sense is the first cause of this world-illusion.

745.   If one is able to remove the ego-sense by means of one's awakened intelligence, he cleanses from his consciousness the impurity known as world-appearance.

746.   The men of wisdom perceive that the entire creation is hidden in the ego-sense.

747.   If the I-ness or ego-sense ceases in you, you will remain like the space and there will be peace.

748.   The ego-sense that perceives the diversity is the creator of the division. The ego-sense is bondage and its cessation is liberation. It is so simple.

749.   "I am the body" is delusion, not truth. You are the pure Self or undivided consciousness.

750.   The notion of "I" is utter ignorance; it blocks the path to liberation.

751.   When a dream-object perishes, nothing is lost: when "the world" or "the I" is lost, nothing is lost.

752.   The abandonment of ego-sense is the cessation of ignorance; this and nothing else is liberation.

753.   The ego-sense is unreal though it appears to be real.

754.   On examination, even the body, etc. are seen to be unreal and false. When even the mind has ceased with the cessation of notions concerning the body and the world, the Self or the infinite consciousness alone remains.

755.   Matter and mind are identical; and both are false. You are deluded by this false appearance. Self-knowledge will dispel this delusion. Both Self-knowledge and the cessation of world-appearance are the characteristics of wisdom.

756.   In the infinite and unmodified or unconditioned consciousness modification is impossible; the conditioning is but a false notion. Therefore, it melts away in the heart of one who has Self-knowledge and who is free from delusion and ego-sense.

757.   To the wise there is neither ego-sense nor the world.

758. The Self alone is real, devoid of the concepts of time, space and such other notions; the Self is not a void. This truth is realized only by those who are established in the supreme state, not by those who rest in the ego-sense.

759. Human beings are narrow-minded and petty minded, interested in the trivia of life. They spend most of their time in pursuit of evil desires.

760. They are tempted away from the path of order and wisdom by their own vanities and desires.

761. Among human beings there are liberated ones. But they are extremely rare.

762. Though the body is experienced to be real, it does not exist in truth.

763. You are not this little personality.

764. Limitless is this ignorance with countless branches in all directions; it cannot come to an end by any means other than Self-knowledge.

765. "I am not a wave, I am the ocean" – when thus the truth is realized, the wave-ness ceases.

766. The mind itself appears to be the objects of perception, just as in dream.

767.   The physical or material universe does not exist at any time anywhere. The subtle body itself appears to be the solid body on account of the notion of such solidity arising in it repeatedly. Its very source is unreal.

768.   For one who rests in his own Self and rejoices in the Self, in whom cravings have ceased and ego-sense is absent, life becomes non-volitional and there is perfect purity. One in millions, however, is able to reach this unconditioned state of pure being.

SRI SANKARA
(769 – 785)

769.   This body is the product of food, and constitutes the material sheath. It depends on food and dies without it. It is a mass of skin, flesh, blood, bones and uncleanness. It is not fit to see as oneself, who is ever pure.

770.   One's true Self shines forth again when the contamination is removed.

771.   Eliminate completely your self-identification with this body, and with determination see that your mind is devoted to the removal of all ideas of additions to your true Self.

772.   So long as even a dreamlike awareness of yourself as an individual in the world remains, as a wise person persistently see to the removal of all ideas of additions to your true Self.

773.   The tendency to see "me" and "mine" in the body and the senses, which are not oneself, must be done away with by the wise by remaining identified with one's true Self.

774.   The wise who have experienced reality call the mind ignorance.

775.   The sage who stands in the Eternal, the Self of being, ever full, of the secondless bliss of the Self, has none of the hopes fitted to time and space that make for the formation of a body of skin, and flesh, subject to dissolution.

776.   Drawing near to the eternal, stainless awakening, whose nature is bliss, put very far away this disguise whose nature is inert and foul.

777.   Outward attachment arises through sensual objects; inward attachment, through personality. Only he who, resting in the Eternal, is free from passion, is able to give them up.

778.   There is no other danger for him who knows, but this wavering as to the Self's real nature. Thence arises delusion, and thence selfish personality; thence comes bondage, and therefrom sorrow.

779.   Bringing to an end the activity of the selfish personality, all passion being laid aside when the supreme object is gained, rest silent, enjoying the bliss of the Self, in the Eternal, through the perfect Self, from all doubt free.

780.   When the false self ceases utterly, and the motions of the mind caused by it come to an end, then, by discerning the hidden Self, the real truth that "I AM THAT" is found.

781.   When free from the grasp of selfish personality, he reaches his real nature; Bliss and Being shine forth by their own light.

782.   Man's circle of birth and death comes through the fault of attributing reality to the unreal, but this false attribution is built up by mind; this is the effective cause of birth and death and sorrow.

783.   Man's circle of birth and death is built by mind, and has no permanent reality.

784.   There is no unwisdom, except in the mind, for the mind is unwisdom, the cause of the bondage to life; when this is destroyed, all is destroyed; when this dominates, the world dominates.

785.   Thinking things not Self are "I" – this is bondage for a man; this, arising from unwisdom, is the cause of falling into the weariness of birth and dying.

STEP FOUR

Increase your desire for liberation. Make your desire for liberation more intense than the energy of a trillion stars. Make your desire for liberation so intense that your entire life is dedicated to awakening.

The desire for liberation is:
(a – e)

a. *The desire to bring the impostor self to its final end.*

b. *The desire to remain eternally as the true Self that is Infinite-Eternal-Awareness-Love-Bliss free of all types of suffering.*

c. *The desire to awaken from the human dream.*

d. *The desire to live eternally in the direct experience of the absolute Self that has never known falsehood, suffering or illusion and that has never changed in all eternity.*

e. *The desire to be forever free from the false and live eternally in the true.*

SRI ANNAMALAI SWAMI
(786 – 788)

786.   The desire for enlightenment is necessary because without it you will never take the necessary steps to realize the Self. A desire to walk to a particular place is necessary before you take any steps. If that desire is not present, you will never take the first step. When you realize the Self, that desire will go.

787.   If the intensity to know yourself is strong enough, the intensity of your yearning will take you to the Self.

788.   Your most important objective must be realizing the Self. If you have not done this, you will spend your time in ignorance and illusion.

SRI SADHU OM
(789 – 792)

789.   The mind which has obtained a burning desire for Self-attention, which is Self-inquiry, is said to be the fully mature one.

790.   Since this mind, which has very well understood that the consciousness which shines as 'I' alone is the source of full and real happiness, now seeks Self because of its natural craving for happiness, this intense desire to attend to Self is indeed the highest form of devotion.

791.   In order to qualify as an aspirant, one must have the absolute conviction that happiness, the sole aim of all living beings, can be obtained not from external objects but only from one's own inmost Self. When one has this qualification, an intense yearning will arise in one's heart to try to attend to and know Self. Indeed, for a true aspirant the desire and effort to know Self will become the most important part of his life, and all other things will be regarded as being only of secondary importance. When such an intense yearning arises in one, success is assured, for 'where there is a will there is a way'.

792.   Mature aspirants will willingly and without rebelling submit themselves to this magnetic power of the Grace of Self-effulgence. Others, on the other hand, will become extroverted (that is, will turn their attention outwards) fearing the attraction of this power. Therefore, we should first make ourself fit by the intense love to know the Self and by the tremendous detachment of having no desire to attend to any second or third person.

SRI MURUGANAR
(793)

793.   Grace, the Supreme, is rare and unique. There is nothing that resembles it. To make it the object of one's desire is the most virtuous of desires. As all other desires are quenched through the very desire for it, it will shine in the heart spontaneously.

794. Earnestness is the only condition of success.

795. All will happen as you want it, provided you really want it.

796. Want the best. The highest happiness, the greatest freedom

797. Your earnestness will determine the rate of progress.

798. It is enough to stop thinking and desiring anything, but the Supreme.

799. The idea of enlightenment is of utmost importance. Just to know that there is such a possibility changes one's entire outlook.

800. If you are truly earnest and honest, the attainment of reality will be yours.

801. Whatever name you give it: will, or steady purpose, or one-pointedness of the mind, you come back to earnestness, sincerity, honesty. When you are in dead earnest, you bend every incident, every second of your life to your purpose. You do not waste time and energy on other things. You are totally dedicated, call it will, or love, or plain honesty.

802. We are complex beings, at war within and without. We contradict ourselves all the time, undoing the work of yesterday. No wonder we are stuck. A little of integrity would make a lot of difference.

803. The desire to find the Self will be surely fulfilled, provided you want nothing else. But you must be honest with yourself and really want nothing else. If in the meantime you want many other things and are engaged in their pursuit, your main purpose may be delayed until you grow wiser and cease being torn between contradictory urges. Go within, without swerving, without ever looking outward.

804. Merely to trust is not enough. You must also desire. Without desire for freedom of what use is the confidence that you can acquire freedom? Desire and confidence must go together. The stronger your desire, the easier comes the help.

805. The greatest Guru is helpless as long as the disciple is not eager to learn.

806. Eagerness and earnestness are all-important. Confidence will come with experience. Be devoted to your goal.

807. If your desire and confidence are strong, they will operate and take you to your goal, for you will not cause delay by hesitation and compromise.

808. The greatest Guru is your inner Self. Truly, he is the supreme teacher. He alone can take you to your goal and he alone meets you at the end of the road. Confide in him and you need no outer Guru. But again you must have the strong desire to find him and do nothing that will create obstacles and delays. And do not waste energy and time on regrets. Learn from your mistakes and do not repeat them.

809. Stop imagining, stop believing. See the contradictions, the incongruities, the falsehood and the sorrow of the human state, the need to go beyond.

810. Freedom can not be gained nor kept without will-to-freedom. You must strive for liberation; the least you can do is uncover and remove the obstacles diligently. If you want peace you must strive for it.

811. All you need is a sincere longing for reality.

812. Questioner: How does one reach the Supreme State?

Maharaj: By renouncing all lesser desires. As long as you are pleased with the lesser, you cannot have the highest.

813. Until you realize the unsatisfactoriness of everything, its transiency and limitation, and collect your energies in one great longing, even the first step is not made.

814. Once you have grasped the truth that the world is full of suffering, that to be born is a calamity, you will find the urge and the energy to go beyond it.

815. There must be the desire first. When the desire is strong, the willingness to try will come. You do not need assurance of success when the desire is strong.

816. Suffering has made you dull, unable to see its enormity. Your first task is to see the sorrow in you and around you; your next to long intensely for liberation. The very intensity of longing will guide you; you need no other guide.

817. Questioner: How is the person removed?

Maharaj: By determination. Understand that it must go and wish it to go – it shall go if you are earnest about it.

818. As long as you are interested in your present way of living you will not abandon it. Discovery cannot come as long as you cling to the familiar. It is only when you realize fully the immense sorrow of your life and revolt against it, that a way out can be found.

819. The real is, behind and beyond words, incommunicable, directly experienced, explosive in its effect on the mind. It is easily had when nothing else is wanted.

820. Abandon your latent tendencies even as a bird wishing to fly into the sky breaks out of its shell. Born of ignorance, these tendencies are hard to destroy, and they give birth to endless sorrow. It is this ignorant self-limiting tendency of the mind that views the infinite as the finite. However, even as sun dispels mist, inquiry into the nature of the Self dispels this ignorant self-limiting tendency. In fact, the very desire to undertake this inquiry is able to bring about a change. Austerities and such other practices are of no use in this. When the mind is purified of its past by the arising of wisdom it abandons its previous tendencies. The mind seeks the Self only in order to dissolve itself in the Self. This indeed is in the very nature of the mind. This is the supreme goal; strive for this.

821. Even as darkness disappears on turning towards light, ignorance disappears if you turn towards the light of the Self. As long as there does not arise a natural yearning for Self-knowledge, so long this ignorance or mental conditioning throws up an endless stream of world-appearance.

822. There arises the pure wish to attain liberation. This leads to serious inquiry. Then the mind becomes subtle because the inquiry thins out the mental conditioning. As a result of the rising of pure wisdom, one's consciousness moves in the reality. Then the mental conditioning vanishes and there is non-attachment. Bondage to actions and their fruits ceases. The vision is firmly established in truth and the apprehension of the unreal is weakened. Even while living and functioning in this world, he who has this unconditioned vision does what has to be done as if he is asleep, without thinking of the world and its pleasures. After some years of living like this, one is fully liberated and he transcends all these states; he is liberated while living.

823. The Self being one and undivided, there is nothing else worth attaining or desiring. This Self undergoes no change and does not die.

824. In this world all things come into being and perish and therefore there is repeated experience of sorrow. All the pleasures of the world inevitably end in sorrow.

825. By Self-knowledge rid yourself of the problems connected with the life hereafter. There is no time to lose for life is ebbing away all the time.

826. When one is knocked about by the troubles and tribulations of earthly existence and is "tired of all this", he seeks refuge from all this.

827. One should carefully investigate the bliss of liberation and the sorrow inevitable to ignorance.

828. Liberation confers "inner coolness" (peace) on the mind; bondage promotes psychological distress. Even after realizing this, one does not strive for liberation. How foolish people are! Such people are overcome by desire for sense-gratification. But even they can cultivate a desire for liberation by a study of this scripture.

SRI SANKARA
(829 – 852)

829. Internal renunciation and external renunciation – it is the dispassionate man who is capable of these. The dispassionate man abandons fetters internal and external because of his yearning for liberation.

830. When the force of the desire for the Truth blossoms, selfish desires wither away, just like darkness vanishes before the radiance of the light of dawn.

831. By achieving the purity of an habitual discrimination and dispassion, the mind is inclined to liberation, so the wise seeker after liberation should first develop these.

832.   If you really have a desire for liberation, avoid the senses from a great distance, as you would poison, and continually practice the nectar-like qualities of contentment, compassion, forbearance, honesty, calm and restraint.

833.   The wise talk here of four qualities, possessed of which one will succeed, but without which one will fail.

First is listed discrimination between unchanging and changing realities, and after that dispassion for the enjoyment of the fruits of action both here and hereafter, and then the group of six qualities including peace and of course the desire for liberation.

834.   Dispassion is the turning away from what can be seen and heard and so on in everything which is impermanent.

835.   The settling of the mind in its goal, by turning away from the mass of objects through observing their defects again and again, is known as peace.

836.   The establishment of the senses each in its own source by means of turning away from their objects is known as control. The supreme restraint is in the mind function not being involved in anything external.

837.   Bearing all afflictions without retaliation and without mental disturbance is what is known as patience.

838. It is in a man who has strong dispassion and desire for liberation that peacefulness and so on are really fruitful.

839. Among the contributory factors of liberation, devotion stands supreme, and it is the search for one's own true nature that is meant by devotion.

840. The practice of faith, devotion and meditation are declared by scripture to be the means to liberation for a seeker after liberation. He who perseveres in these will achieve freedom from bondage to the body, created by ignorance.

841. Let all those who put away and cast aside every sin of thought, who are sated with this world's joys, whose thoughts are full of peace, who delight in words of wisdom, who rule themselves, who long to be free, draw near to this teaching, which is dedicated to them.

842. Renouncing inwardly, renouncing outwardly – this is possible only for him who is free from passion; and he who is free from passion renounces all attachment within and without, through the longing for freedom.

843. Four perfections are numbered by the wise. When they are present there is success, but in their absence is failure.

    First is counted the discernment between things lasting and unlasting. Next Dispassion, the indifference to self-indulgence. Then the six graces, beginning with restfulness. Then the longing for freedom.

844.   A certainty like this – the eternal is real, the fleeting world is unreal; this is that discernment between things lasting and unlasting.

845.   And this is dispassion – a perpetual willingness to give up all sensual self-indulgence – everything lower than the eternal, through a constant sense of their insufficiency.

846.   Then the six graces: a steady intentness of the mind on its goal; this is restfulness.

847.   The steadying of the powers that act and perceive, each in its own sphere, turning them back from sensuality; this is self-control.

848.   The raising of the mind above external things; this is the true withdrawal.

849.   The enduring of all ills without petulance and without self-pity; this is right endurance.

850.   The intentness of the soul on the pure eternal; this is right meditation.

851.   When dispassion and longing for Freedom are strong, then restfulness and the other graces will bear fruit.

852.   But when these two – dispassion and longing for freedom – are lacking, then restfulness and the other graces are a mere appearance.

Be inspired, encouraged and motivated to: 1. Make and maintain the decision to bring the impostor self and all suffering to its final end and thus remain forever in infinite-awareness-love-bliss. 2. Actually practice all seven steps.

SRI RAMANA MAHARSHI
(853 – 900)

853. What does one gain, you may well ask, by giving up the wealth immense of worldly pleasure and seeking only mere Awareness? The benefit of true Awareness is the unbroken prevalence of peace within the heart, the bliss of one's own natural being.

854. Unfailing immortality accrues only to those who have destroyed the ego whose demon-dance obstructs the vision of the precious truth that we are ever-perfect Being-Awareness-Bliss.

855. Imagining that this newcomer, the body, is oneself, one thinks that one is born and that one dies. The moment this delusion goes one's own true immortality is gained.

856. Death is nothing but the fond delusion that this newcomer, the body, is oneself. When the ego, the clinging to delusion, ends, the ensuing bliss of true Awareness, being one without a second, this, this only is immortality.

857.   True clearness, freedom from the mind's ripples and shadows, this alone is ever-fresh immortality. By this awareness pure, by this alone and by no other means, can death, mere delusion, end.

858.   Mind's dissolution in the Self, the ocean of Awareness, this is peace eternal. The Heart's vast space, the love-filled ocean of Bliss supreme, is the true I.

859.   Illusion gone, one with the Self, he knows only bliss supreme.

860.   For those who seek eternal life the assurance stands: the senses five retracted tortoise-like, the mind turned homeward to the Self and there abiding is pure bliss.

861.   Do not dwell in the desert hot of the non-self, eating arid sand. Come into the Heart, the mansion cool, shady, vast, serene and feast on the bliss of Self.

862.   The vision of truth destroying false illusion, is like a swelling ocean of blissful grace. And in this silence of Self-awareness beyond thought, there is no fall, no failure.

863.   Those whose body-bound ego is dead live a life of pure Awareness, rejoicing in the Self, carefree, in peace unruffled by desire.

864. What is That forgetting which we have fallen under the power spell of this false world? Unless we know That, the Real, there is no chance whatever for the death and disappearance of our pain.

865. Fond, foolish mind afflicted by desire for transient pleasures in this world and the next, if you stand tranquil, still, you're sure to gain the freedom, the transcendent bliss beyond these two worlds.

866. Though in this false world one may live on, the ending of both "I" and "mine" in the clarity of true awareness void of every doubt, this only is abidance in the bliss of being That.

867. Worth pursuing is Self-inquiry, worth enjoying is the Self's infinitude. Worth giving up is the ego-sense. To end all sorrow the final refuge is one's source, the Self of pure Awareness.

868. The deeds we do in dream touch not our waking life, but slip away when we awake. Even so, our deeds done in this clouded ego-life disappear and leave no trace when we wake up in the divine white light of Self-awareness.

869. One whirls and turns, pines in sore pain in this false dream world, till at last the sleeper in his soft bed wakes up, the bad dream ends, one feels relieved, untouched, free as the pure white screen. Such freedom is Self-knowledge pure.

870.   Let no one seek to gain good ends regardless of the means employed. If the means are evil, they corrupt the intended good. Therefore make sure that means are ever wholly pure.

871.   Returning to the source from which we have emerged, we are restored to our own true Being. Enjoying there bright and clear our natural bliss, still, still, unmoving we abide.

872.   Since it was one's own past effort that now has ripened into fate, one can with greater present effort change one's fate.

873.   Not an iota of the past can touch those who dwell unceasingly in the firmament of Self-awareness vast, boundless, frontierless and full.

874.   If without wasting time one starts and keeps up steady Self-inquiry, one's life becomes at once ennobled, one is no more this wretched body and there wells up within one's heart a sea of bliss supreme.

875.   Swerve not from your true state, thinking some thought. But if you do, commit not the same folly. Do nothing that you later may regret. Even if you did once, never repeat it.

876.   O mind, you wander far in search of bliss not knowing your natural state of Freedom. Your home of infinite bliss you will regain if only you go back the way you came.

877. A superstructure raised without a strong foundation soon collapses in disgrace. Hence earnest seekers first ensure by every means their own stern self-discipline through devotion and detachment.

878. After we have renounced whatever can be renounced, That which abides, and cannot be renounced, is True Being shining in the Heart, the fount, the flood of Bliss.

879. By practice of Self-inquiry sharpen the weapon divine of silence. With this dig out, uproot and cast away the weed, the ego. Thus can be released the fount of bliss serene.

880. A woman with a necklace round her neck imagines it is lost, and after long search elsewhere touches her own neck and there finds it; even so, the Self is here within. Probe for it there and find it.

881. Our real Being, the sun that never can see the darkness of illusion, knows no trace of pain or suffering. Misery is what one brings upon oneself by fondly thinking that one is the body, not the Self.

882. The goal, the Truth, is Self-awareness. Reaching it is annihilation of the painful illusion of birth.

883. Knowledge absolute is free from all the differences created by the false, deluding ego. The gracious stillness, the awareness all-transcendent, is the state supreme experienced by the Great.

884.   When the intellect withdrawn from questing after outward objects returns to its own natural home, the Heart, our Being-Awareness-Bliss, restored to us, abides for ever.

885.   The miserable, proud ego thinks that bliss is found in pleasing objects; and if it dies, the Self abides as the sole Bliss.

886.   There never is non-being for the Self which is Awareness pure. When relative knowledge ends, when false, conceptual duality is no more, the Self whose Being is Awareness does not cease to be.

887.   Non-dual infinite Awareness where the error of seeing, hearing, knowing various objects has been destroyed, this is the purest bliss serene.

888.   When the false notion "I am the body" dies, what abides is what's worth having, the vast, bright, silent void, the Self. Why is it so? Because in truth the only state free from all pain and all desire is pure Self-Being.

889.   Bliss is the very nature of the Self. Self is the infinitude of Bliss. All Being is but Bliss. Knowing this firmly, in the Self abide enjoying Bliss for ever.

890.   The Self, the home of blissful Awareness, is an ocean vast of peace serene. And he whose mind turns inward and dives deep within it, gains the infinite treasure of its grace.

891. The ever-present Self, the radiant gem, this is the rarest, richest treasure. Look within and find and hold it fast. Your penury, the grand illusion, source of every trouble on earth, will vanish forthwith.

892. In the flawless state of Being the Self, without a sense of "I" or "mine", the still abidance in and as Awareness pure, this is the noblest victory worth winning.

893. Only when the Self is gained is permanent, perfect, blissful peace attained.

894. The darkness of illusion never touches the seer who knows his true identity as Awareness pure, vast as the sky, bright as the sun. Only the blind who think they are bodies suffer from dark ignorance.

895. Life you desire. But how to live you know not. Thinking that this sinking deep in this void, vain, illusive waking-dream is "life", you proudly claim you "live". Pierce this illusion, go, grasp the Truth, eternal life.

896. That Heart which truly knows the Self is full of love whence Bliss supreme wells up for ever.

897. The only goal worth seeking is the bliss supreme of Self-awareness.

898. The sage enjoys as his own being the bliss of all transcendent Being. The error lies in these ignorant folk seeing him as a body that suffers.

899.   The sage abiding in Self-being, asleep and yet awake, immersed in the still, deep, immutable ocean of bliss supreme, will never lapse back into this ruinous world and suffer.

900.   When the mad craving for false, trivial objects is no more, and the ego is in its source absorbed and lost, the life of Self-awareness true that now shines forth is bliss supreme.

SRI MURUGANAR
(901 – 914)

901.   Through inner renunciation, free of all desires except for the lofty desire for the flood of divine grace, purity arose within my soul, and as my mind, becoming perfectly pure, conducted its inquiry, the greater life of grace that nothing can mar, the reality of the Self, manifested within my heart.

902.   Established in the highest awareness, which is of the nature of the indivisible Self, and which is free of a discriminating consciousness based upon discursive thought, my mind's illusory cravings have ceased, and that enervated state dominated by suffering and deluded desire has come to its final end.

903.   Through the arrogance of the body-bound ego, my mind rushed hither and thither until it was finally and irrevocably defeated, as my consciousness merged into that glorious unbroken awareness that is the bliss of being, which is the boundless expanse of the one true Self.

904.   Attaining a vision beyond the reach of sight and an awareness more subtle than the tiniest atom, I have become established in the reality of the Self that shines unaffected by anything else.   And thus my mind has merged with the supreme in which there is no going, no coming, no connection with anything whatsoever.

905.   In the supreme that exists as the Self, free of all modification, the movements of my own mind, realizing their true nature in the heart as that radiant supreme, entirely subsided, remaining absorbed in the Self as the Self.

906.   Through being established in the being-awareness that is my authentic nature, I became free of the mental activity that caused me to act in accordance with the imaginary creations of a divided mind that was deluded by the thought of 'I' and 'this'.

907.   My mind's activity along with my ego subsided and fell into total abeyance so that, with no longer anything to experience or know, I rejoiced with the nature of the eternal and all-pervading Self as my sole object.

908. The eye of truth which abides as unalloyed consciousness, pure grace possessing power and beauty, is indeed the absolute, the infinite eye.

909. We have learned to see only those things that seem to be real, but will not learn to see the truth of the one that sees and knows them. If we do grasp the reality of the one that perceives and knows, the ghost-like ego will fall away and the deep intense bliss of the life of grace, the supreme Self, will come into existence.

910. Reality, the supreme and unique nature of the Self, is nothing other than the heart in which the power of the mind to generate its false creations has died. If the aggressive ego is eliminated at its source, a joy will arise that the sorrows of the mind cannot touch.

911. Those who, through holy grace, have purified their consciousness by remaining as the witness, will attain an awareness whose strength derives from its one-pointedness. Through that awareness they will be freed from delusive desires and the terrors they bring, thus attaining the authentic state of supreme bliss free of all affliction.

912. Laying hold of that Self, which is the cause of love, you should realize your true nature in the bliss of the Real.

913. Eliminating the error of my words, thoughts and deeply flawed ego-mind so that all my defects subsided, a greater existence enfolded me, the wealth of the Real, flaring up within my heart in the form of dynamic consciousness.

914. Mistaking dream for reality, my changeful mind had been overspread by dark clouds of delusion, intoxicated by its own error until it was submerged in the reality of the immutable Self and merged into a true existence where all conflict is absent.

SRI SADHU OM
(915 – 920)

915. The truth is that you yourself are happiness! Happiness is your true nature! You are not this body-form! You are full and perfect bliss itself!!

916. Where there is happiness, there is love!

917. Until perfect happiness is obtained, do not give up your efforts. Know the way to experience always and uninterruptedly that happiness which is you, and which exists and shines within you as your real nature.

918. The efforts of worldly people lead only to a fleeting semblance of happiness, whereas this effort of an aspirant – Self-inquiry – paves the path to perfect, eternal and unlimited happiness.

919. The experience of Self-knowledge is the very pinnacle of happiness.

920.   Why has it been said that one ought to make effort repeatedly to be in that state (our existence-consciousness) and ought to abide in it with more and more love? Because, until all the tendencies which drive one out of it are completely exhausted, this state will seem to come and go. Hence the need for continued effort and love to abide in the Self.

SRI ANNAMALAI SWAMI
(921 – 930)

921.   You have to make an enormous effort to realize the Self. It is very easy to stop on the way and fall back into ignorance. At any moment you can fall back. You have to make a strong determined effort to remain on the peak when you first reach it, but eventually a time will come when you are fully established in the Self. When that happens, you cannot fall.

922.   You must have a lifelong commitment to establish yourself in the Self. Your determination to succeed must be strong and firm, and it should manifest as continuous, not part-time, effort. For many lifetimes you have been immersed in ignorance. You are habituated to it. All your deeply rooted beliefs, all your patterns of behavior reinforce ignorance and strengthen the hold it has over you. This ignorance is so strong, so deeply enmeshed in all your psychological structures, it takes a massive effort over a long period of time to break free from it. The habits and beliefs that sustain it have to be challenged again and again.

923. Don't be discouraged by the length of the journey, and don't slacken in your efforts to get home.

924. The Self always remains as it is – as peace, without birth, without death.

925. Questioner: Is Swamiji totally established in the Self?

Annamalai Swami: Yes.

926. The Self is peace and happiness.

927. Don't waste energy on thinking or evaluating how well or how badly you are doing in your meditation.

928. Keep your body in good condition if you want to, but don't ever believe that it is you. You can keep your car in good working order without ever believing you are the car. Have the same attitude towards your body. Both will perish, but the Self will continue because it is always there. When you identify with transient things that pass away or perish, you too will pass away and perish, but when you identify with the Self, you will not pass away or change in any way. The Self has no birth, no death, no bondage, no misery, no youth, no old age, and no sickness. These are attributes of changing bodies and minds, not the Self. Be the Self and none of these things will ever happen to you.

929.   Questioner: Is there still work to be done after the Self is reached and experienced?

Annamalai Swami: Initially, abidance in the Self may not be firm and irreversible. Vigilance may be needed at first to maintain it.

930.   Self has no birth, no death, no sufferings and no problems.

SRI NISARGADATTA MAHARAJ
(931 – 992)

931.   We discover it by being earnest, by searching, inquiring, questioning daily and hourly, by giving one's life to this discovery.

932.   To know the Self as the only reality and all else as temporal and transient is freedom, peace and joy.

933.   What helps to know yourself is right.   What prevents, is wrong. To know one's real Self is bliss, to forget – is sorrow.

934.   In seeking you discover that you are neither the body nor mind, and the love of the Self in you is for the Self in all. The two are one. The consciousness in you and the consciousness in me, apparently two, really one.

935.   Steady faith is stronger than destiny. Destiny is the result of causes, mostly accidental, and is therefore loosely woven.   Confidence and good hope will overcome it easily.

936.   Action is a proof of earnestness. Do what you are told diligently and faithfully and all obstacles will dissolve.

937.   Be fully aware of your own being and you will be in bliss consciously.

938.   You are love itself.

939.   You must be eager to see. You need both clarity and earnestness for Self-knowledge. You need maturity of heart and mind which comes through earnest application in daily life of whatever little you have understood.

940.   Don't look for quick results; there may be none within your noticing.

941.   I am infinite peace and silence in which nothing appears.

942.   The real peace cannot be disturbed.

943.   Find yourself first and endless blessings will follow.

944.   Wake up, know yourself, be yourself.

945. Whatever you may hear, see, or think of, I am not that.

946. I was not, am not, shall not be a body.

947. The very facts of repetition, of struggling on and on and of endurance and perseverance, in spite of boredom and despair and complete lack of conviction are really crucial.

948. There is nothing wrong in repeating the same truth again and again until it becomes reality.

949. I am neither the body, nor the experiencer of the body.

950. I was never born. How can I grow old? What I appear to be to you exists only in your mind. I am not concerned with it.

951. What matters is that I am neither the body nor the mind.

952. Compassion and love are my very core.

953. To me nothing ever happens. There is something changeless, motionless, immovable, rock-like, unassailable; a solid mass of pure being-consciousness-bliss. I am never out of it.

954. On your side there is so much trouble. On mine there is no trouble at all. Come to my side.

955.   You are quite capable of crossing over. Only be sincere.

956.   Laziness and restlessness often stand in the way and until they are seen and removed, the progress is slow.

957.   Integrity will take you to reality.

958.   When all the false self-identifications are thrown away, what remains is all-embracing love.

959.   The very nature of the Self is love.

960.   It is a matter of actual experience that the Self has being independent of mind and body. It is being-awareness-bliss. Awareness of being is bliss.

961.   Since you are neither body nor mind, destiny has no control over you. You are completely free.

962.   You are accusing me of having been born – I plead not guilty!

963.   You are not the body. You are the immensity and infinity of consciousness.

964.   Beyond the mind there is no suffering.

965.   Earnestness is the golden key.

966.   What the mind invents, the mind destroys. But the real is not invented and cannot be destroyed. Hold on to that over which the mind has no power.

967.   Faith is not blind. It is the willingness to try.

968.   Questioner: What is the experience which comes nearest to the Supreme?

Maharaj: Immense peace and boundless love.

969.   You must be extreme to reach the Supreme.

970.   You are pure being-awareness-bliss.

971.   The only happiness worth the name is the natural happiness of conscious being.

972.   I am complete and perfect. I am the beingness of being, the knowingness of knowing, the fullness of happiness.

973.   Try and try again.

974.   If only they go deeply into the fact of being and discover the vastness and the glory to which the 'I am' is the door, and cross the door and go beyond, their life will be full of happiness and light.

975.   There is nothing wrong with you as the Self.

976.   The real is simple, open, clear and kind, beautiful and joyous.

977.   First return to your true being and then act from the heart of love.

978.   Just turn away from all that occupies the mind; do whatever work you have to complete, but avoid new obligations; keep empty, keep available, resist not what comes uninvited. In the end you reach a state of non-grasping, of joyful non-attachment, of inner ease and freedom indescribable, yet wonderfully real.

979.   However heavy may be the hand of destiny, it can be lifted by patience and self-control. Integrity and purity remove the obstacles.

980.   That which is alive in you is immortal.

981.   The task seems hopeless until suddenly all becomes clear and simple and so wonderfully easy. But, as long as you are interested in your present way of living, you will shirk from the final leap into the unknown.

982.   The real is bliss supreme.

983.   No external activity can reach the inner Self; worship and prayers remain on the surface only; to go deeper meditation is essential, the striving to go beyond the states of sleep, dream and waking. In the beginning the attempts are irregular, then they recur more often, become regular, then continuous and intense, until all obstacles are conquered.

984.   By all means wish yourself well. Think over, feel out deeply what is really good for you and strive for it earnestly. Very soon you will find that the real is your only good.

985.　The inner happiness is overwhelmingly real.

986.　Do not be afraid of freedom from desire and fear. It enables you to live a life so different from all you know, so much more intense and interesting, that, truly, by losing all you gain all.

987.　Questioner: There must be some hopeless cases too?

Maharaj: None is hopeless. Obstacles can be overcome.

988.　Relinquish your habits and addictions, live a simple and sober life, don't hurt a living being; this is the foundation of Yoga. To find reality you must be real in the smallest daily action; there can be no deceit in the search for truth.

989.　It is your self-identification with the body, which, of course, is limited in space and time, that gives you the feeling of finiteness. In reality you are infinite and eternal.

990.　Try. One step at a time is easy. Energy flows from earnestness.

991.　There is a vastness beyond the farthest reaches of the mind. That vastness is my home; that vastness is myself. And that vastness is also love.

992.　Love is boundless.

THE SUPREME YOGA
(993 – 1209)

993.   Whatever be the external appearance of the liberated sage, his wisdom remains unchanged. The difference is only in the eyes of the ignorant spectator.

994.   Self-effort is of two categories: that of past births and that of this birth. The latter effectively counteracts the former.

995.   There is no power greater than right action in the present. Hence, one should take recourse to self-effort.

996.   One should never yield to laziness but strive to attain liberation, seeing that life is ebbing away every moment.

997.   By self-effort acquire wisdom and then realize that this self-effort is not without its own end, in the direct realization of the truth.

998.   The present is infinitely more potent than the past. They indeed are fools who are satisfied with the fruits of their past effort and do not engage themselves in self-effort now.

999.   The Holy ones emphasize: persistently tread the path that leads to the eternal good.

1000. Renounce fatalism and apply yourself to self-effort.

1001. You are indeed consciousness itself, not inert physical matter.

1002. The tendencies brought forward from past incarnations are of two kinds – pure and impure. The pure ones lead you towards liberation, and the impure ones invite trouble.

1003. You are free to strengthen the pure latent tendencies in preference to the impure ones.

1004. By encouraging the good tendencies to act repeatedly, strengthen them. The impure ones will weaken by disuse.

1005. Bliss is possible only by Self-knowledge, not by any other means. Hence, one should apply oneself constantly to Self-knowledge.

1006. In order to cross this formidable ocean of repetitive history, one should resort to that which is eternal and unchanging. He alone is the best among men whose mind rests in the eternal and is, therefore, fully self-controlled and at peace.

1007. He who wears the armor of self-control is not harmed by sorrow.

1008. In the light of inquiry, there is realization of the eternal and unchanging reality; this is the supreme.

1009. The infinite consciousness is forever in infinite consciousness.

1010. If one's intelligence is established in this truth concerning the infinite consciousness, it reaches the supreme state of liberation. This depends upon one's own intensity of self-effort.

1011. The Self is empty like space; but it is not nothingness since it is consciousness.

1012. When this illusory division is not seen for what it is, there is the arising of the false egotism. But when the mind inquires into its own nature, this division disappears. There is realization of the one infinite consciousness, and one attains great bliss.

1013. Whatever might have been the origin of the mind and whatever it might be, one should constantly direct it towards liberation, through self-effort.

1014. Abandon your imperfect vision which is not based on fact; rest in the perfect vision which is of the nature of bliss and which is based on truth.

1015. The Self is not destroyed when the body falls.

1016. Victory over this goblin known as mind is gained when with the aid of one's own self-effort one attains Self-knowledge and abandons the craving for what the mind desires as pleasure.

1017. By intense self-effort it is possible to gain victory over the mind.

1018. Mind constantly swings like a pendulum between the reality and the appearance, between consciousness and inertness. When the mind contemplates the inert objects for a considerable time, it assumes the characteristic of such inertness. When the same mind is devoted to inquiry and wisdom, it shakes off all conditioning and returns to its original nature as pure consciousness. Mind takes the very form of that which one contemplates, whether it is natural or cultivated. Therefore, resolutely but intelligently contemplate the state beyond sorrow, free from all doubts. The mind is capable of retraining itself; there is indeed no other way.

1019. Rest in the Self.

1020. To the enlightened vision, only the infinite consciousness exists, naught else. Do not become an ignorant man; become a sage. Destroy the mental conditioning that gives rise to this world appearance. Why do you, like an ignorant man, consider this body as your self and feel miserable?

1021. When the body dies, the Self does not die.

1022. By attaining knowledge of the Self which is infinite consciousness, you will go beyond grief, delusion, birth and death.

1023. The Self which is not grasped by the senses is not touched by sorrow.

1024. One should resort to that which is not limited, conditioned or finite.

1025. Abandon the notions of 'I' and 'this' and remain established in the truth.

1026. The conditioned mind experiences suffering; when rid of the conditioning, it experiences delight.

1027. One should not set foot on the wrong path even in times of great distress.

1028. Wake up from the slumber of ignorance.

1029. Zealous effort should be directed towards Self-knowledge alone.

1030. When the mind's conditioning ceases, then ignorance, craving, desires and aversions, delusion, stupidity, fear and ideations come to an end; purity, auspiciousness and goodness arise. One enjoys the delight of Self-knowledge.

1031. I am the fullness. I am the Self-bliss.

1032. Constantly seek to discover the supreme peace.

1033. He who exerts seriously now is able to overcome predispositions and exalt himself from the states of darkness and stupidity and impurity.

1034. There is nothing that intense self-effort cannot achieve.

1035. Ignorance of the Self is the cause of your sorrow; knowledge of the Self leads to delight and tranquility.

1036. One should constantly endeavor to awaken the mind which dwells in the body in order that one may go beyond the process of becoming – for such becoming is fraught with sorrow.

1037. Be free from distress. Be free of duality.

1038. Rest in the inner silence.

1039. Be free from all mental perversions and from the blinding taint of illusion. Rest content in your own Self. Thus, be free from all distress. Remain in an expansive state in the Self, like the full ocean. Rejoice in the Self by the Self.

1040. One should enjoy the delight that flows from peace.

1041. When the heart is established in peace, there arises the pure bliss of the Self.

1042. O unsteady mind! This worldly life is not conducive to your true happiness. Hence, reach the state of equanimity. It is in such equanimity that you will experience peace, bliss and the truth. Whenever you create perverse thinking in yourself, out of your wantonness, it is then that this world-illusion begins to expand and spread out. It is when you entertain desire for pleasure that this world-illusion sprouts countless branches. It is thought that gives rise to this network of world-appearance. Hence, abandon this whim and fancy and attain to equanimity.

1043. Whatever sorrows there may be that seem to be difficult to overcome are easily crossed over with the help of the boat of wisdom (the inner light). He who is devoid of this wisdom is bothered even by minor difficulties. But, he who has this wisdom, even if he is alone and helpless in this world and even if he is unlearned in the scriptures, easily crosses the sea of sorrow. Even without the help of another, the man of wisdom accomplishes his work; he who is without wisdom does not, nay even his capital is lost. Hence, one should constantly endeavor to gain this inner light or wisdom, even as one who aspires for fruits exerts constant effort in his garden. Wisdom is the root which, when thus constantly nourished, yields the good fruits of Self-knowledge. The effort and the energy that are directed by the people in worldly activities should first be directed to the gaining of this wisdom.

1044. When the infinite Self is realized, sorrow comes to an end, even the seeds of delusion are destroyed, the shower of misfortune ceases, and the perception of evil ends.

1045. Seek only that which is not limited or finite.

1046. You are the eternal, infinite light, pure and extremely subtle.

1047. True dispassion does not arise in one by austerity, charity, pilgrimage, etc. but only by directly perceiving one's own nature. And, there is no means for direct Self-realization except right self-exertion.

1048. I am the eternal subject free from all object and predicate. I salute that omnipresent consciousness which is free from the tempting concept of objects, and hence eternally free.

1049. I am limitless like space.

1050. You are the infinite.

1051. I am pure consciousness. I am peace beyond thought.

1052. I am the omnipresent.

1053. The delights of even countless worlds is nothing compared to the bliss of the Self. He who has nothing but has this Self-knowledge has everything. He who abandons this and seeks other things is not a man of wisdom.

1054. This Self alone is to be sought, adored and meditated upon.

1055. This Self is the eternal existence.

1056. I, the Self, alone am: in me there is no percept or concept.

1057. O Self, free from the mire of ego-sense, salutations to you.

1058. O Self, in whom the lotus of bliss has fully blossomed, salutations to you.

1059. O Self, the sun that dispels the darkness of ignorance in the heart, salutations to you.

1060. The past tendencies, mental conditioning and limitations have been completely destroyed. I begin to wonder: how was it that for such a long time I was caught up in the trap of the ego-sense! Freed from dependency, from habits of thought, from desires and cravings, from deluded belief in the existence of the ego, from the coloring of pleasure-seeking tendency, and from revelry – my mind has reached a state of utter quiescence. With this, all sorrow has come to an end and the light of supreme bliss has dawned!

1061. Salutations to my Self which is infinite and egoless: salutations to the formless Self.

1062. Abandon vanity, anger, impurity and violence: for great souls are not overcome by such base qualities.

1063. I am delighted. I am in a state of utter equilibrium and of supreme peace. I stand unmoving. I have reached Self-knowledge.

1064. Be established in the consciousness of undivided oneness.

1065. Birth and death are mental concepts: they have nothing to do with the Self.

1066. All mental weaknesses come to an end by self-effort.

1067. What now remains is the pure consciousness which is free from the shadow of doubt. I am the infinite Self.

1068. You shine radiant with bliss, with peace, with sweetness and with purity.

1069. One should uplift oneself and not revel in the mire of ignorance.

1070. You are not born when the body is born, nor do you die when it dies.

1071. When the cravings drop away, one experiences great bliss and supreme peace within oneself. The sage of Self-knowledge attains courage and stability and shines in his own glory. He enjoys supreme satisfaction in himself. He is enlightened and this inner light shines brightly within him.

1072. By their own self-effort millions of beings have attained liberation.

1073. It is only by steady practice that one is freed from sorrow and experiences the bliss of the Self.

1074. I am free and happy.

1075. I am the eternal Self that is omnipresent and subtle. I have reached that state of reality which is unreflected in anything, which is beginningless and endless and which is utterly pure.

1076. Liberation is attained only by wisdom or Self-knowledge. Only through such wisdom does one go beyond sorrow, destroy ignorance and attain perfection.

1077. There is freedom from all experiences.

1078. However difficult it may be to reach this state, strive for it.

1079. Strive to get established in that supreme state.

1080. They who reach that state which is pure and undecaying and which is the truth of one's own Self, attain to supreme peace.

1081. Self-knowledge alone bestows delight on you. A man of Self-knowledge alone lives. Hence, gain Self-knowledge.

1082. Recollect your essential nature as the infinite consciousness. Abandon the notions of diversity. You are what you are: nay, not even that as a concept but beyond it, you are the Self-luminous being. Salutations to you, O cosmic being that is infinite consciousness.

1083. Remain in a state of total equanimity. You are like the infinite space.

1084. I rest in supreme peace.

1085. It is absence of Self-knowledge that is known as ignorance or delusion. When the Self is known one reaches the shores of limitless intelligence.

1086. Again and again I repeat all this for the sake of your spiritual awakening; the realization of the Self does not happen without such repetition (or, spiritual practice).

1087. When the whirlpool dies in the water, nothing is dead!

1088. The ripples play on the surface of the ocean, they are neither born nor do they die!

1089. I have nothing to do with sorrow, with actions, with delusion or desire. I am at peace, free from sorrow.

1090. I am that pure consciousness in which the pure intelligence functions without thought-interference.

1091. The consciousness indwelling all beings is the same – that consciousness I am.

1092. I have attained that consciousness which is the indweller of all; which, though it is all, is yet beyond the diversity.

1093. I am fully awakened to the reality. My delusion has vanished.

1094. I rest peacefully in the state of one who is liberated even while living.

1095. The best of all states, O sage, is indeed the vision of the one infinite consciousness. Even the contemplation of the Self which is infinite consciousness banishes sorrow, terminates the long-dream vision of the world-appearance, purifies the mind and the heart, and dispels worries and misfortunes. That contemplation of the Self is devoid of mentation.

1096. This is the Self, it is pure infinite consciousness.

1097. One should abandon the false dependence on divine intervention which is in fact the creation of the immature childish mind and, with one's intense self-effort one should gain mastery over the mind.

1098. Even as when a statue is broken, no life is lost, when the body born of thoughts and notions is dead, nothing is lost. It is like the loss of the second moon when one is cured of diplopia. The Self which is infinite consciousness does not die nor does it undergo any change whatsoever.

1099. Once the infinite consciousness is realized, the clouds of ignorance are banished for ever.

1100. Consciousness, which is purer than space, does not perish.

1101. I am that infinite Self which is indivisible; I remain full and infinite.

1102. I remain established in the Self.

1103. I have realized the fullness of direct Self-knowledge.

1104. When you rest on the pinnacle of Self-knowledge, it is unwise to fall into the pit of ego-sense again. Let hopes cease and let notions vanish, let the mind reach the state of no-mind while you live unattached. You are bound only when you are ignorant. You will not be bound if you have Self-knowledge. Hence, strive by every means to remain vigilant in Self-knowledge.

1105. Even as an error of yesterday can be rectified and turned into a good action by self-effort today, the habits of the past can be overcome by appropriate self-effort.

1106. Behold the Self which is infinite, unmanifest, eternal and which is of the nature of pure consciousness and untainted. You are unborn and eternal!

1107. The unreal has no existence and the real does not cease to be.

1108. The delusion of body, etc. and sorrow, etc. vanish upon spiritual awakening.

1109. Be established in oneness. You are the single ocean of consciousness.

1110. Do not entertain the feeling of "This is self or consciousness" towards what is not-self. When the body perishes, nothing is lost. The Self is never lost! The Self is by definition the indestructible and infinite consciousness.

1111. The bodies have an end, but the Self (the infinite consciousness) is eternal.

1112. Previous impressions are destroyed only by intense self-effort. Even if the mountains were pulverized and the worlds dissolved, one should not give up self-effort.

1113. Sorrow ceases, all the bondages are rent asunder and doubts are dispelled when one is fully established in the equanimity of the Self for a long time, when the perception of division has ceased and when there is the experience of fullness through the knowledge of that which is to be known. What is to be known? It is the Self which is pure and which is of the nature of pure consciousness which is omnipresent and eternal.

1114. I am free from all delusion. I am at peace.

1115. I remain rooted in that which is truth, not in the appearance.

1116. I experience the greatest joy in remaining established in the reality that shines in my heart.

1117. I delight in the Self.

1118. The Self is neither the doer nor the action nor the instrument. It is the truth. It is the eternal absolute consciousness. It is Self-knowledge.

1119. The infinite consciousness alone exists.

1120. Remain well established in peace and tranquility, free from mental conditioning.

1121. The transcendental reality is eternal.

1122. My delusion is gone.

1123. When pure awareness arises, all notions subside. There is perfection.

1124. One alone is, the pure consciousness. Nothing in the three worlds is ever born or dies. The infinite consciousness alone exists.

1125. There is only one infinite consciousness.

1126. Like the limitless space, I remain in the unconditioned state.

1127. The Self is not affected by the fate of the body.

1128. I am peace.

1129. I am free from confusion and delusion.

1130. You are that subtle and pure consciousness which is indivisible, free from ideation.

1131. I am now established in the transcendental state.

1132. Behold the Self-luminous Self.

1133. You are that infinite consciousness.

1134. Dive deep into the inner peace, not in the sea of diversity.

1135. The unreal does not come into being at any time, nor does the reality or the Self ever cease to be.

1136. I am swimming in the ocean of bliss. I am the indivisible Self which is the supreme Self.

1137. That is the state of bliss which is infinite consciousness. Immerse yourself in that ocean of nectar which is full of peace; do not drown in diversity.

1138. Steady your mind by practice.

1139. Remain forever what you are in truth.

1140. Remain at peace in silence.

1141. Remain in the pure Self.

1142. Immortality is attained only by the knowledge of the reality. There is no other means.

1143. In the Self which is infinite consciousness there is no movement at all.

1144. You are THAT, that has neither birth nor death.

1145. When the veils that hide the truth are removed, the truth shines by itself.

1146. In the spiritually awakened and enlightened state the sage rests in the Self.

1147. Cling to the pillar of Self-knowledge, knowing the Self to be free from old age and death.

1148. I am firmly established in the pure non-dual and indivisible consciousness which is the supreme state.

1149. I am the pure space-like consciousness devoid of objective experience and beyond all mental activity or thought. I am the pure and infinite consciousness. Even so are you.

1150. I am pure consciousness and nothing but that.

1151. The pure undivided consciousness alone exists.

1152. One should rest in the inner peace.

1153. The life stream of the knower of truth flows in harmony, while the life stream of the ignorant is full of whirlpools.

1154. Consciousness is eternal and unconditioned.

1155. I do not perceive the ego-sense, etc. but I realize the existence of the pure consciousness or absolute peace.

1156. The wayfarer does not despair at the sight of the long road ahead but takes one step at a time.

1157. There is nothing other than unconditioned consciousness.

1158. When one moves away from one's real nature there is great sorrow; when one rests in the Self there is great peace.

1159. The Self or the infinite consciousness does not do anything and is not involved in activities.

1160. Resting in the Self is supreme good.

1161. The reality is infinite consciousness.

1162. Perception of the reality is the best form of worship.

1163. Wisdom reveals consciousness as the Self.

1164. Remain as the pure consciousness. Drink the essence of Self-knowledge. Rest free from all doubts in the garden of liberation.

1165. What does exist after this appearance is rejected, is in fact the truth. But it has no name! Like a lion, break away from this cage of ignorance and rise above everything. To abandon the notions of "I" and "mine" is liberation.

1166. Liberation is peace. Liberation is extinction of all conditioning. Liberation is freedom from every kind of physical, psychological and psychic distress.

1167. The man of Self-knowledge is awake to that which is non-existent to the ignorant. That which is real to the latter is non-existent to the enlightened.

1168. The wise man radiates wisdom and goodness. Then seeking to free himself from the cage of ignorance, he flies away from pleasure towards the unconditioned bliss.

1169. This is the only path to salvation: one should be totally devoted to the one desirable cause, one should be instructed in the right effort for its attainment and one should again and again engage oneself in such right action. By the right effort ignorance is dispelled and the ignorant become enlightened.

1170. By persistent effort, the impossible becomes possible.

1171. Only by persistent and determined self-effort and by one's own direct experience is perfection attained, not by any other means.

1172. On account of this realization of the truth, the delusion concerning the material or physical ceased in me. In its place there was the great consciousness which neither rises nor sets. There was awareness in which I saw neither space nor the rock but I was aware of only the infinite.

1173. There is only one consciousness which is unborn and tranquil.

1174. I have not been created at all and I do not see anything.

1175. Infinite, indivisible consciousness alone is the reality.

1176. Infinite consciousness is pure existence at all times and it does not undergo any diminution. It shines by its own light, it has no beginning nor middle nor end.

1177. The only reality is the infinite consciousness.

1178. The infinite consciousness alone exists.

1179. I exist but I am unborn.

1180. You are pure and supreme consciousness.

1181. After a long time I have attained egolessness.

1182. The innermost being of everyone which is pure consciousness is unchanging.

1183. When one feels "I am the body", he forfeits strength and wisdom; he who realizes "I am pure consciousness" gains them.

1184. One should stand firm in one's own realization without being distracted nor deflected.

1185. I am pure consciousness and so are you.

1186. There is no possibility for the existence of another other than consciousness. When the body perishes, consciousness does not perish.

1187. One should engage oneself seriously in the realization of the Self.

1188. One surely gains that for which one strives; if one neglects it he loses it. The mind flows along the course of wisdom or of ignorance, in whichever direction you make it flow.

1189. The powers gained through contemplation, etc. can be seen by others; but the state of liberation that one attains cannot be seen by others.

1190. Even if a hundred bodies perish, consciousness does not perish.

1191. Only the knowers of the truth (the sages of Self-knowledge) experience no sorrow at all.

1192. There is only one formless, beginningless, endless, non-dual infinite consciousness.

1193. Consciousness always shines pure.

1194. The infinite consciousness is absolutely pure.

1195. To us who are enlightened there is no creation, no death or cessation; all is for ever unborn and peaceful.

1196. In that pure consciousness there is no sorrow nor death.

1197. The supreme state is not attained without effort.

1198. Consciousness alone exists in consciousness.

1199. The infinite consciousness is devoid of body.

1200. Consciousness is ever free.

1201. By awakening, awakening is attained.

1202. Just as the nightmare and the sorrow caused by it cease when one wakes up, the sorrow caused by the perception of the world-illusion ceases when one wakes up from that illusion.

1203. I am free from doubt. I am free. I am blissful. I am as I am as the infinite.

1204. Wonderful is this supreme peace. What is to be gained has been gained. The perception of the objects has been abandoned. True enlightenment has dawned and it shall never set again.

1205. The knowers of truth rest in the infinite consciousness alone.

1206. I have attained supreme purity; all the impurities have cleared away. All my misunderstandings and delusions have been dispelled.

1207. I am full of bliss which is eternal and undiluted.

1208. Deluded experience does not cease until one resorts to the right means of liberation and attains awakening.

1209. Remain established in the reality, in the state of enlightenment.

1210. I am free, I am bodiless, I am without sex and indestructible. I am at peace; I am infinite, without blemish and eternal.

1211. I am not the doer and I am not the reaper of the consequences. I am unchanging and without activity. I am pure awareness by nature; I am perfect and forever blessed.

1212. I am eternal, undivided, actionless, limitless, unattached – perfect awareness by nature.

1213. I have no master and I am without any sense of "me" and "mine."

1214. I am beyond contamination.

1215. I am boundless.

1216. I am actionless, changeless, partless, formless, imageless, endless and supportless – one without a second.

1217. I am perfect indivisible awareness and I am infinite bliss.

1218. There is no satisfaction or elimination of suffering through the experience of unreal things, so experience that non-dual bliss and remain happily content established in to your own true nature.

1219. Experience the supreme peace of silence through your true nature composed of that non-dual bliss.

1220. For the man who has recognized his own nature and who is enjoying the experience of inner bliss, there is nothing that gives him greater satisfaction than the peace that comes from having no desires.

1221. I can neither see, hear or experience anything else there, as it is I who exist there by myself with the characteristics of Being and Bliss.

1222. You too should recognize this supreme Truth about yourself, your true nature and the essence of bliss, and shaking off the illusion created by your own imagination, become liberated, fulfilled and enlightened.

1223. The fruit of dispassion is understanding, the fruit of understanding is imperturbability, and the fruit of the experience of bliss within is peace.

1224. Tranquility is the supreme satisfaction, leading to incomparable bliss.

1225. Come to the eternally pure reality of consciousness and bliss and reject afar identification with this dull and unclean body.

1226. Stop thinking about anything which is not your true Self, for that is degrading and productive of pain, and instead think about your true nature, which is bliss itself and productive of liberation.

1227. Restrain speech within. Restrain the mind in the understanding and restrain the understanding in the consciousness that observes the understanding. Restrain that in the perfect and imageless Self, and enjoy supreme peace.

1228. The wise man should always strive for the cessation of thought.

1229. The wise man knows the perfect joy of the letting go of everything, and experiences the attainment of the overwhelming bliss of Reality.

1230. Because of the diversity of the things he identifies himself with, a man tends to see himself as complex, but with the removal of the identification, he is himself again and perfect as he is.

1231. The supreme Self is the internal reality of Truth and Bliss, eternally indivisible and pure consciousness.

1232. There is no other way to the breaking of the bonds of temporal existence for the seeker after liberation than the realization of his own true nature.

1233. In real purity the qualities which occur are contentment, Self-understanding, supreme peace, fulfillment, joy and abiding in one's supreme Self, through which one experiences real bliss.

1234. The Self is ever blissful and never experiences suffering.

1235. No one can free someone else from bondage.

1236. Abandoning all actions and breaking free from the bonds of achievements, the wise and intelligent should apply themselves to Self-knowledge.

1237. By this discourse of Teacher and Pupil, the character of the Self is taught to those seeking Freedom, that they may be born to the joy of awakening.

1238. When there is direct perception, the Self shines forth clearly, without regard to place or time or rites of purification.

1239. The knower of the Eternal, freed from bondage, most excellent, gains the victory.

1240. This knower of the Eternal, ever bodiless, things pleasant or painful touch not at all, nor things fair or foul.

1241. Without act am I, without change, without division, without form; without wavering am I, everlasting am I, resting on naught else, and secondless.

1242. I transcend all; there is none but me. I am pure, partless awakening, I too am unbroken bliss.

1243. I have done what was to be done, freed am I from the grasp of the sorrowing world. My own being is everlasting bliss; I am filled full, through the favor of the Self.

1244. Unbound am I, formless am I, without distinction am I, no longer able to be broken; in perfect peace am I, and endless; I am stainless, immemorial.

1245. I am in nature pure awakening.

1246. I am the one essence of everlasting bliss, the real, the secondless Eternal.

1247. Thus dwelling in the supreme Eternal, through the real Self, he stands and beholds naught else. From the knowledge that I am the Eternal, the accumulated works, heaped up even through hundreds of myriads of ages, melt away like the work of dream, on awaking.

1248. One, verily, is the Eternal, without a second. There is no difference at all. Altogether perfect, without beginning or end, measureless and without change.

1249. The home of Being, the home of Consciousness, the home of Bliss enduring, changeless; one, verily, without a second, is the Eternal.

1250. The fullness of Being, Self-perfect, pure awakened, unlike aught here; one, verily, without second, is the Eternal.

1251. They who have cast away passion, who have cast away sensual delights, peaceful, well-ruled, the sages, the mighty, knowing reality in the supreme consummation, have gained the highest joy in union with the Self.

1252. Thou worthy one also, seeking this higher reality of the Self, whose whole nature is the fullness of bliss, washing away the delusions thine own mind has built up, be free, gaining thy end, perfectly awakened.

1253. Through soul-vision, through the Self utterly unshaken, behold the Self's reality, by the clear eye of awakening.

1254. Knowing the Self through one's own realization, as one's own partless Self, and being perfected, let him stand firm in the unwavering Self.

1255. I taste the glory of the ocean of the Supreme Eternal, filled full of the ambrosial bliss of the Self.

1256. The supreme end is the incomparable enjoyment of the Self's bliss.

1257. In soul-vision the wise man perceives in his heart a certain wide-extending awakening, whose form is pure bliss, incomparable, the other shore, for ever free, where is no desire, limitless as the ether, partless, from wavering free, the perfect Eternal.

1258. In soul-vision the wise man perceives in his heart the unfading, undying reality.

1259. Entering the purified inner organ into the witness whose nature is the Self, who is pure awakening, leading upward step by step to unmoving firmness, let him then gain vision of perfection.

1260. "I am the Eternal"; knowing this clearly, those whose minds are awakened, who have abandoned the outward, becoming the Eternal, dwell in the Self, which is extending consciousness and bliss.

1261. Enjoyment of perpetual bliss belongs to the Self that is free.

1262. Renounce the illusion of self-dwelling in the body; center the consciousness on the Self. Thou art the seer, thou art the stainless, thou art in truth the supreme, secondless Eternal.

1263. With powers of sense controlled enter in ecstasy into the hidden Self, with mind at peace perpetually.

1264. When purified by the power of uninterrupted intentness, the mind is thus melted in the Eternal, then ecstasy is purified of all doubt, and of itself enjoys the essence of secondless bliss.

1265. Through this ecstasy comes destruction of the knot of accumulated mind-images, destruction of all works; within and without, for ever and altogether.

1266. He who thus understands, discerning the real from the unreal, ascertaining reality by his own awakened vision, knowing his own Self as partless awakening, freed from these things reaches peace in the Self.

1267. Resting in the Eternal brings joy by experiencing it, and takes away the supreme sorrow that we feel, whose cause is unwisdom.

1268. The wise man may enter into that joy-bringing treasure.

1269. Eternal, unfading joy, unstained – this is the Eternal, THAT THOU ART.

1270. This shines out unchanging, higher than the highest, the hidden one essence, whose character is Selfhood, reality, consciousness, joy, endless unfading – this is the Eternal, THAT THOU ART.

1271. He who through the Self dwells here in the secret place, for him there is no coming forth again to the world of form.

1272. There is no other path of freedom from the bondage of the world but knowledge of the reality of his Self, for him who would be free.

1273. The Eternal, the secondless bliss, is gained by the awakened.

1274. The wise who has become the Eternal does not return again to birth and death.

1275. The real, wisdom, the endless, the Eternal, pure, supreme, Self-perfect, the one essence of eternal bliss, universal, undivided, unbroken – this he gains.

1276. This is the real, supreme, secondless, for besides the Self no other is; there is nothing else at all in the condition of perfect awakening to the reality.

1277. Eternal blissful Self-consciousness; know that as the Self here in the heart.

1278. The Self shines forth pure, the one essence of eternal bliss, beheld within, supreme, Self-luminous.

1279. Separating from the congeries of things visible the hidden Self within, which is detached, not involved in actions, and dissolving all in the Self, he who stands thus, has attained liberation.

1280. Through this knowledge of the Self supreme he shall destroy this circle of birth and death and its root together.

1281. The Self itself is perpetual bliss.

1282. With all earnest effort to be free from the bondage of the world, the wise must strive themselves.

1283. Let the wise one strive after Freedom, giving up all longing for sensual self-indulgence.

STEP SIX

Turn your attention inward.

SRI RAMANA MAHARSHI
(1284 – 1304)

1284. With mind turned inward, drown the world in the great void, dispel illusion. Beholding then the void as void, destroy the void by drowning it in the deep ocean of Self-Awareness.

1285. Those well established in the Self will never pursue the world's vile ways. For such descent into the false allurements of the world is yielding to the animal weakness for sense-pleasure.

1286. Not in one single thing on earth can happiness be found. How could the muddled mind delude itself and think that happiness can be derived from objects in this world?

1287. Fond, foolish people may find joy in pleasure at the moment. Soon it palls and leaves but pain behind.

1288. Those who desire and like and live the trivial life the ego knows reject as if it were unreal the natural life of infinite bliss within their own hearts ever present for their enjoyment.

1289. Those who enjoy the ego's life of false phenomena perish and die. The state of grace, supreme Awareness, the life lived in Self-Being, this alone is bliss worth seeking.

1290. Poor seer who suffer endlessly because you still perceive the object, not the subject, please look inward, not without, and taste the bliss of non-duality.

1291. Running out in search of wonders and dancing there with pleasure, do not perish. Better with the light of grace, look, look within, and find certitude in being and biding as your true Self.

1292. Those who diving deep within have found the Self have nothing else to know. And why? Because they have gone themselves beyond all forms and are Awareness without form.

1293. Investigating who perceives this false external world of sense, bring to an end the frisking ego's mischief. Abiding as supreme awareness in the heart, this alone is liberation.

1294. One who has through supreme devotion gained one's true Being as Awareness can recognize no other state except this; one's natural state of being one supreme Awareness.

1295. Sense-pleasures sought and found by blind, unguarded fools are fit only for contempt by those who long to taste the rich, ripe fruit of Bliss supreme immeasurably sweet.

1296. Absence of mental craving for sense-enjoyments is true fasting. Abidance in the Self is worship true, hence, those with pure, clear wisdom cherish as most precious this fasting and this worship.

1297. Better the state of inner peace and Self-abidance where no thought arises than attainment of the power to bring about fulfillment, prompt and sure, of every wish.

1298. Since That which Is shines bright within as I, the Self is but Awareness. To search in the heart and find the Self, the best help is the inescapable light of the one Self alone.

1299. The world should not occupy one's mind.

1300. The wise renounce at heart and quite forget the wondrous charms of this false world which only ruins those who trust it.

1301. That which is for ever shines in grace as I, the Self, the Heart. Can That be blamed for lacking Grace? The fault is theirs who do not turn within and seek the Self in love.

1302. The universal eye avoids no creature. We are blind, for we look outward, not within.

1303. Those who have known the Self aright, instead of wandering in the world, abide in their own natural state.

1304. This worldly life of false phenomena full of fear is sinking deeper in illusion, not authentic living.

1305. Questioner: The outside world is a miserable, confusing place. There is not much going on there that helps us to remember who we really are.

Annamalai Swami: Yes, you can say that this state of affairs is also Bhagavan's grace, Bhagavan's compassion. You could say that He keeps the world like this as an incentive to go inwards. This state of affairs sets up a real choice; if we go outwards there are problems; if we go inwards there is peace.

1306. We have to give up all the things of this world, and all other worlds, and direct all our attention towards the Self. If we want anything in this world or the next our energy will be dispersed in these desires, and to fulfill these desires we shall have to be reborn again and again.

1307. You are going to different places on a pilgrimage, but what you are really looking for is you yourself. You cannot achieve success in this by going on external searches because you yourself are the one that is being looked for. Your real nature is peace. Forgetting this, you have lost your peace and you are searching in the outside world where there is no peace to be found.

1308. To find the Self, to find what is real, you have to look inside yourself.

1309. Mind is not improved by long journeys to far-flung places. Instead, make an internal pilgrimage. Take the mind back to its source and plunge it into the peace-giving waters of the Self. If you once make this pilgrimage, you will never need to go looking for happiness or peace in any other place.

1310. If you are not able to find this Self within yourself, you will not find it anywhere else. Searching on the outside and visiting holy places will not help you.

1311. Many people are visiting swamis, temples and holy places. Doing these things will not yield any good fruit. For real and lasting results you have to look inside yourself and discover the Self within. You can do that anywhere.

1312. Turn to the light within all the time.

1313. You dissipate your desire for the Self by undertaking all kinds of useless activities that waste your time and lead to attachments. You think that your life is endless and that you can put off meditation till a later date. With this kind of attitude, you will die filled with regrets, not filled with peace.

1314. The more we attend to thoughts pertaining to the second and third persons, the more they will increase.

1315. There are two kinds of impediments which act as obstacles for the mind to achieve Self-abidance, and hence two kinds of strength of mind are essential for overcoming them. The first strength is that which is required to prevent the mind from branching out into innumerable thoughts through the force of tendencies towards the sense-objects. The second strength is that which is required to direct the mind (the power of attention) towards the first person or Self, that is, the strength actually to attend to Self.

1316. The nature of the mind is to attend always to things other than itself, that is, to know only second and third persons. If the mind in this way attends to a thing, it means that it is clinging (attaching itself) to that thing. Attention itself is attachment!

1317. When the power of attention of the mind is directed more and more towards second and third person objects, both the strength to attend to those objects and the ignorance – the five sense-knowledges in the form of thoughts about them – will grow more and more.

1318. The mind which attends to Self is no more the mind; it is the consciousness aspect of Self! Likewise, so long as it attends to the second and third persons (the world), it is not the consciousness aspect of Self; it is the mind.

1319. Many are those who take qualified experiences of taste, light, sound and so on to be the final attainment of Self-knowledge and because they have had these experiences they think that they have attained liberation and they become more and more entangled in attention to second and third persons, thus losing their foothold on Self-attention. Such aspirants are called 'those fallen from yoga.' This is similar to a man bound for Delhi getting down from the train at some intermediate station, thinking 'Verily, this is Delhi', being deluded by its attractive grandeur!

1320. A sincere aspirant should arrange his work in such a way that he will spend only a portion of his time and energy for maintaining the body, so that he can utilize the remaining time and energy in striving to earn the great profit of Self-knowledge.

SRI MURUGANAR
(1321 – 1324)

1321. When we mistake that which is impermanent for that which is enduring, it only serves to emphasize the disharmony within our hearts. The true temperament is one that cleaves to the indestructible Self dwelling at the heart of our very existence as the immovable reality.

1322. Unless the mind subsides into the heart, whose nature is consciousness, and experiences the deep peace of union with it, the mind, through separation from it, will fall into the trap of the sense organs, be whirled about in the world of the senses, and become scattered.

1323. Those who crave a worldly life of pomp and ostentation, relying on the fleeting impressions of the sense organs, will remain slaves to the obscuring desires of the flesh, and give scant regard to the eternal life of living as the supreme.

1324. Those who, instead of enjoying the bliss of the Heart – the form of consciousness – embrace and find pleasure in the objects of sense, will wander from birth to death and death to birth, alternating in that deluded consciousness between the states of remembering and forgetting.

SRI NISARGADATTA MAHARAJ
(1325 – 1367)

1325. I see what you too could see, here and now, but for the wrong focus of your attention. You give no attention to your Self. Your mind is all with things, people and ideas, never with your Self. Bring your Self into focus, become aware of your own existence.

1326. True happiness cannot be found in things that change and pass away. Pleasure and pain alternate inexorably. Happiness comes from the Self and can be found in the Self only.

1327. Pain is the background of all your pleasures. You want them because you suffer. On the other hand, the very search for pleasure is the cause of pain. It is a vicious circle.

1328. It is all a matter of focus. Your mind is focused in the world; mine is focused in reality.

1329. Deliberate daily exercise in discrimination between the true and the false and renunciation of the false is meditation.

1330. Look to yourself for the permanent. Dive deep within and find what is real in you.

1331. The world is the abode of desires and fears. You cannot find peace in it. For peace you must go beyond the world.

1332. To know the world you forget the Self – to know the Self you forget the world. What is world after all? A collection of memories. Cling to one thing, that matters, hold on to 'I am' and let go all else.

1333. The Self is beyond both, beyond the brain, beyond the mind.

1334. If you leave it to time, millions of years will be needed. Giving up desire after desire is a lengthy process with the end never in sight. Leave alone your desires and fears, give your entire attention to the subject, to him who is behind the experience of desire and fear.

1335. Turn within and you will come to trust yourself.

1336. Nothing stops you but preoccupation with the outer which prevents you from focusing the inner.

1337. Sooner or later you are bound to discover that if you really want to find, you must dig at one place only – within.

1338. Playing with various approaches may be due to resistance to going within, to the fear of having to abandon the illusion of being something or somebody in particular. To find water you do not dig small pits all over the place, but drill deep in one place only. Similarly, to find your Self you have to explore yourself.

1339. The world is full of contradictions, hence your search for harmony and peace. These you cannot find in the world, for the world is the child of chaos. To find order you must search within.

1340. What happens to the body and the mind may not be within your power to change, but you can always put an end to your imagining yourself to be body and mind. Whatever happens, remind yourself that only your body and mind are affected, not yourself.

1341. To eschew the unnecessary is austerity.

1342. Having things under control at all times is austerity.

1343. It is the choices you make that are wrong. To imagine that some little thing – food, sex, power, fame – will make you happy is to deceive yourself. Only something as vast and deep as your real Self can make you truly and lastingly happy.

1344. Your difficulty lies in your wanting reality and being afraid of it at the same time. You are afraid of it because you do not know it. The familiar things are known, you feel secure with them.

1345. As long as your focus is on the body, you will remain in the clutches of food, sex, fear and death. Find yourself and be free.

1346. Abandon all ideas about yourself and you will find yourself to be the pure witness, beyond all that can happen to the body or the mind.

1347. The body and the mind are only symptoms of ignorance, of misapprehension.

1348. As long as the mind is busy with its contortions, it does not perceive its own source.

1349. By its very nature the mind is outward turned; it always tends to seek for the source of things among the things themselves; to be told to look for the source within, is, in a way, the beginning of a new life.

1350. Renunciation of the false is liberating and energizing. It lays open the road to perfection.

1351. It is the clinging to the false that makes the true so difficult to see.

1352. When you want something, ask yourself: "Do I really need it?" and if the answer is no, then just drop it.

1353. Freedom comes through renunciation. All possession is bondage.

1354. Maharaj: Stay with the changeless among the changeful, until you are able to go beyond.

Questioner: When will it happen?

Maharaj: It will happen as soon as you remove the obstacles.

Questioner: Which obstacles?

Maharaj: Desire for the false and fear of the true.

1355. Questioner: In the beginning we may have to pray and meditate for some time before we are ready for Self-inquiry.

Maharaj: If you believe so, go on. To me, all delay is a waste of time. You can skip all the preparation and go directly for the ultimate search within. Of all the Yogas it is the simplest and the shortest.

1356. The innermost light, shining peacefully and timelessly in the heart, is the real Guru.

1357. I know myself as I am – timeless, spaceless, causeless. You happen not to know, being engrossed as you are in other things.

1358. Limit your interests and activities to what is needed for you and your dependents barest needs. Save all your energies and time for breaking the wall your mind had built around you.

1359. All you need is already within you, only you must approach your Self with reverence and love.

1360. Now, go within, into a state which you may compare to a state of waking sleep, in which you are aware of yourself, but not of the world. In that state you will know, without the least trace of doubt, that at the root of your being you are free and happy.

1361. The clarification and purification needed at the very start of the journey, only awareness can give. Love and will shall have their turn, but the ground must be prepared. The sun of awareness must rise first – all else will follow.

1362. Awareness is always with you. The same attention that you give to the outer, you turn to the inner. No new or special kind of awareness is needed.

1363. As long as you are engrossed in the world, you are unable to know yourself: to know yourself, turn away your attention from the world and turn it within.

1364. You must seek the Self and, having found it, stay with it.

1365. The body and the mind are limited and therefore vulnerable; they need protection which gives rise to fear. As long as you identify yourself with them you are bound to suffer; realize your independence and remain happy. I tell you, this is the secret of happiness. To believe that you depend on things and people for happiness is due to ignorance of your true nature; to know that you need nothing to be happy, except Self-knowledge, is wisdom.

1366. The world appears to you so overwhelmingly real, because you think of it all the time; cease thinking of it and it will dissolve into thin mist.

1367. Self-awareness is Yoga.

THE SUPREME YOGA
(1368 – 1410)

1368. None of the objects in this world is meant to give happiness to anyone. The mind vainly seeks to find such happiness in the objects of this world.

1369. This perception of the defects of the world has destroyed the undesirable tendencies in my mind; and therefore, desire for sense-pleasure does not arise in my mind.

1370. I am constantly inquiring: "How can I wean my heart completely away from even thinking of this ever-changing phantasm called the world?"

1371. All that is good and auspicious flows from self-control. All evil is dispelled by self-control.

1372. As long as one is not satisfied in the Self, he will be subjected to sorrow. With the rise of contentment the purity of one's heart blooms.

1373. This Self is neither far nor near; it is not inaccessible nor is it in distant places: it is what in oneself appears to be the experience of bliss, and is therefore realized in oneself.

1374. He who does not allow his mind to roam in objects of pleasure is able to master it.

1375. Ignorance or mental conditioning is acquired by man effortlessly and it seems to promote pleasure, but in truth it is the giver of grief. It creates a delusion of pleasure only by the total veiling of Self-knowledge.

1376. If the mind turns towards the truth, it abandons its identification with the body and attains the supreme.

1377. As long as the objective universe is perceived one does not realize the Self.

1378. One should abandon all cravings for pleasure and attain wisdom. Only the mind that has been well disciplined really experiences happiness.

1379. The reality is the one infinite consciousness which does not undergo any change.

1380. In truth, only the indivisible and unmodified consciousness exists.

1381. They are the true heroes who have brought under control the mind which is dominated by ignorance and delusion.

1382. Rest in peace and purity like the ocean when it is not agitated by wind.

1383. Do not let your mind wander among the objects of the world. You yourself are the supreme Self, the infinite consciousness; you are naught else!

1384. He who runs after the objects created by his own mind surely comes to grief.

1385. In this ocean of ignorant mental conditioning, he who has found the raft of Self-knowledge is saved from drowning; he who has not found that raft is surely drowned.

1386. They who are busy with the diverse affairs in this world in pursuit of pleasure and power, do not desire to know the truth which they obviously do not see.

1387. O mind, abandon your craving for sense-pleasures so that you may be rid of the miseries of repeated old age and death.

1388. The mind is not subdued without persistent practice. Hence, take up this practice of renunciation. Until one turns away from sense-pleasure here, one will continue to roam in this world of sorrow. Even a strong man will not reach his destination if he does not move towards it: no one can reach the state of total dispassion without persistent practice.

1389. When you turn completely away from the pursuit of pleasure, then you attain to the supreme state through the means of inquiry.

1390. I shall give up everything and with my mind completely withdrawn from the pursuit of pleasure, I shall remain happily established in the Self.

1391. Abandon the desire for the essenceless and useless sense-pleasure in this world. The attractive objects that tempt you here do not deserve your admiration.

1392. In whatever the mind tends to sink, retrieve it from it and direct it towards the truth. Thus will the wild elephant of the mind be tamed.

1393. The ghost of delusion afflicts one only as long as Self-knowledge does not arise in him.

1394. Until we attain Self-knowledge, we shall return again to this plane of birth and death to undergo childhood, youth, manhood, old age and death again and again, we shall engage ourselves in the same essenceless actions and experiences. Cravings destroy wisdom. Lost in satisfying sensual appetites, life ebbs away fast.

1395. Suffering flows towards those who are mentally conditioned. This whole creation is thus pervaded by ignorance.

1396. This body can have no relationship whatsoever with the Self.

1397. When one is ignorant, one entertains the wrong notion that the body is the Self; his own senses prove to be his worst enemies.

1398. In the absence of the "taste" (direct knowledge) of the cosmic intelligence, the senses endeavor to apprehend their objects and vainly imagine that such contact gives rise to meaningful experience!

1399. Even as a caged bird is unable to find freedom, the ignorant man devoted to the fulfillment of his appetites is unable to find release from bondage. His mind, which is befuddled with apparently countless tendencies and conditioning is unable to see clearly the revolving wheel of life and death.

1400. In the darkness of ignorance, the fool thinks he experiences pleasure or happiness in the objects of this world.

1401. All these objects have a beginning and an end, they are limited, they are perishable.

1402. Liberation is attained when one arrives at the state of supreme peace after intelligent inquiry into the nature of the Self and after this has brought about an inner awakening.

1403. Awakening of inner intelligence destroys ignorance.

1404. Eternal good is not to be found in any of the activities of any of the senses.

1405. Establish your mind, which flits from one thing too another, firmly in your heart.

1406. The wise one restrains the senses and remains centered in the Self.

1407. The fool who revels in pleasure invites sorrow and misfortune.

1408. The fullness of perfection begins with the effectiveness of self-discipline or the abandonment of the pursuit of pleasure.

1409. It is a great misfortune to pursue pleasure.

1410. Investigate the truth with the help of direct experience; behold the primordial truth by direct experience. One who abandons this experience and runs after illusory "realities" is a fool.

SRI SANKARA
(1411 – 1438)

1411. When he has lost sight of his true Self, immaculate and resplendent, a man identifies himself with his body out of ignorance.

1412. Identification of oneself with the body is the seed of the pain of birth etc. in people attached to the unreal, so get rid of it with care. When this thought is eliminated, there is no more desire for rebirth.

1413. There is no self-identification with such things as the body for a liberated man. There is no being awake for someone asleep, nor sleep for someone awake, for these two states are by their very nature distinct.

1414. A wise man attains peace by recognizing his own true nature as undifferentiated awareness.

1415. Knowing his true indivisible nature by his own realization the perfected man should remain in full possession of himself free from imaginations within.

1416. When the mass of desires for things other than oneself, obscuring the contrary desire for one's real Self, are eliminated by constant Self-remembrance, then it discloses itself of its own accord.

1417. The fruit of knowledge should be the turning away from the unreal, while turning towards the unreal is seen to be the fruit of ignorance.

1418. Established in meditation, with the senses controlled, the mind calmed and continually turned inwards, destroy the darkness of beginningless ignorance by recognizing the oneness of Reality.

1419. To overcome the outward-turning power of the mind is hard to accomplish without completely eliminating the veiling effect, but the covering over one's inner Self can be removed by discriminating between seer and objects.

1420. Absence of an barrier is finally unquestionable when there is no longer any distraction caused by illusory objects.

1421. When the mind loses its direction towards its goal and becomes outward-turned it runs from one thing to another, like a play-ball carelessly dropped on the steps of some stairs.

1422. He who is devoted to meditating on the Truth attains the eternal glory of his true nature, while he who delights in dwelling on the unreal perishes.

1423. Dwelling on externals increases the fruit of superfluous evil desires for all sorts of things, so wisely recognizing this fact, one should abandon externals and cultivate attention to one's true nature within.

1424. As the mind becomes more and more inward-turned, it becomes gradually freed from external desires, and when all such desires are fully eliminated Self-realization is completely freed from obstruction.

1425. Seers know this supreme Reality, free from the distinctions of knower, known and knowledge, infinite, complete in itself and consisting of pure Awareness.

1426. This supreme Reality is non-dual in the absence of any other reality beside itself. In the state of knowledge of ultimate truth there is nothing else.

1427. Completely rooting out desire for the senses and abandoning all activity by one-pointed devotion to liberation, he who is established with true faith in study etc. purges away the passion from his understanding.

1428. The Self itself is pure consciousness.

1429. Through enjoyment of unreal things, there is no contentment at all, nor any getting rid of pain. Therefore contented by enjoying the essence of secondless bliss, stand thou rejoicing, resting on the Self that is true Being.

1430. Attracted by the Self the man goes to the being of the Self by resting on it alone.

1431. Perfect discernment, born of clear awakening, arises free from doubt, and pure of all bondage, where there is no propelling power towards delusive objects, once the division is made between the real natures of the seer and what is seen.

1432. Attachment to the outward brings as its fruit the perpetual increase of evil mind-images. Knowing this and putting away outward things by discernment, let him place his attachment in the Self forever.

1433. He whose delight is attachment to the real, freed, he gains the greatness of the Self, eternal; but he who delights in attachment to the false, perishes.

1434. Transcending every visible object of sense, fixing the mind on pure being, the totality of bliss, with right intentness within and without, pass the time.

1435. The motion of enticement to sensual objects is the cause of world-bondage, through attachment to what is other than Self.

1436. By resting ever in the Self, the restless mind of him who seeks union is stilled, and all imaginings fade away.

1437. As the mind rests more and more on the Self behind it, it is more and more freed from outward imaginings; when imaginings are put away, and no residue left, he enters and becomes the Self.

1438. The knowledge of the real by the eye of clear insight is to be gained by one's own sight and not by the teacher's.

*Spend as much time as you can **every** day practicing
the most rapid, effective and direct method
that brings the impostor self to its final end.*

That method is described in the following quotes:
(1439 – 1574)

SRI RAMANA MAHARSHI
(1439 – 1450)

1439. If you observe awareness steadily, this awareness itself as Guru will reveal the Truth.

1440. Instead of looking outward at objects, you observe that looking.

1441. The only true and full awareness is awareness of awareness. Till awareness is awareness of itself, it knows no peace at all.

1442. True natural awareness which goes not after alien objects is the Heart. Since actionless awareness shines as real Being, its joy consists in concentration on itself.

1443. Not like other things unreal, but always by its Being real, the Self as permanent Awareness has no other dwelling place than its own radiant Awareness.

1444. The Self, our Being, is Awareness.

1445. The method of Self-inquiry is to turn the outward going mind back to its source, the Heart, the Self, and fix it ever there, preventing the rising of the empty "I."

1446. Inquiry is making the mind abide firm in the Self till the false ego, illusion's seed, has perished.

1447. One who has wisely chosen the straight path of Self-inquiry can never go astray; for like the bright, clear Sun, the Self reveals itself direct to whoso turns towards it.

1448. Undeluded by whatever else may come and go, unwinking watch the Self, because the little fault of forgetting for one moment one's true Being as Pure Awareness brings tremendous loss.

1449. If you refrain from looking at this or that or any other object then by that overpowering look into absolute Being you become yourself the boundless space of pure Awareness which alone is real Being.

1450. Unbroken Self-awareness is the true, bright path of devotion or love. Knowledge of our inherent nature as indivisible Bliss supreme wells up as love.

1451. Questioner: But is it enough to be aware of the awareness?

Annamalai Swami: You are repeating the question, so I will repeat the answer. If you remain in the state of consciousness, there will be nothing apart from it. No problems, no misery, no questions.

1452. Ignorance is ignorance of the Self, and to remove it Self-awareness is required. When you come to an awareness of the Self, ignorance vanishes. If you don't lose contact with the Self, ignorance can never arise.

1453. Bhagavan spoke about turning inwards to face the Self. That is all that is needed. If we look outwards, we become entangled with objects and we lose awareness of the Self shining within us. But when, by repeated practice, we gain the strength to keep our focus on the Self within, we become one with it and the darkness of self-ignorance vanishes.

1454. Tayumanuvar, a Tamil saint whom Bhagavan often quoted, wrote in one of his poems:

"My Guru merely told me that I am consciousness. Having heard this, I held unto consciousness. What he told me was just one sentence, but I cannot describe the bliss I attained from holding onto that one simple sentence. Through that one sentence I attained a peace and a happiness that can never be explained in words."

1455. You can only put your attention on one thing at a time. While it is on the mind or the body, it cannot be on the Self. Conversely, if you put attention on the Self and become absorbed in it, there will be no awareness of mind and body.

1456. You have forcibly to drag your wandering attention back to the Self each time it shows an interest in going anywhere else.

1457. While the search was on, that which was being sought was, in reality, that through which the seeing was taking place. You were looking for an object that finally turned out to be the subject that was doing the seeing.

1458. Even the sequence, "To whom has this thought come? To me," is based on ignorance of the truth. Why? Because it is verbalizing a state of ignorance; it is perpetuating an erroneous assumption that there is a person who is having troublesome thoughts. You are the Self, not some make-believe person who is having thoughts.

1459. Clinging to the consciousness 'I' and thereby acquiring a greater and greater intensity of concentration upon it, is diving deep within. Instead of thus diving within, many, thinking that they are engaged in Self-inquiry, sit down for hours together simply repeating mentally or vocally, "Who am I?" or "Whence am I?." There are others again who, when they sit for inquiry, face their thoughts and endlessly repeat mentally the following questions taught by Sri Bhagavan: "To whom come these thoughts? To me; who am I?", or sometimes they even wait for the next thought to come up so that they can fling these questions at it! Even this is futile.

1460. We should not remain watching "What is the next thought?" Merely to keep on questioning in this manner is not Self-attention.

1461. By saying, "This is the direct path for all", Sri Bhagavan points out that anyone, however weak his mind may be, can acquire through this path that true strength of mind which is required to abide in one's source. Therefore, taking to Self-attention, which is the real introversion, is by itself far better than giving any other target to the mind.

1462. If our attention is directed only towards ourself, our knowledge of our existence alone is nourished, and since the mind is not attended to, it is deprived of its strength.

1463. When, through the aforesaid Self-attention, we are more and more firmly fixed in our existence-consciousness, the tendencies will be destroyed because there is no one to attend to them.

1464. The feeling 'I am' is the experience common to one and all.

1465. The pure existence-consciousness, 'I am', is not a thought; this consciousness is our nature. 'I am a man' is not our pure consciousness; it is only our thought!

SRI MURUGANAR
(1466 – 1470)

1466. That which dwells within all that is, that through which awareness itself becomes aware, that which exists in each thing as its individual nature, is the true 'I' that shines as pure consciousness.

1467. The indivisible Reality that dwells within is consciousness itself.

1468. The truth of the Self shines as the pure consciousness underlying the mind. The fitting course is to discern it in the heart through being-consciousness and then to establish it firmly there through deep contemplation, so that the fetters of worldly bondage – the companions of lustful infatuation – disappear, being revealed as false, and liberation, the mark of the Real, shines forth.

1469. Bitter worldly bondage arises through the degrading error of mistaking the Self, being-consciousness-bliss, for the insentient body. It can only be removed through the certainty of the experience of Self-inquiry that is filled with the divine light of consciousness.

1470. Know that the perfectly pure Self will well up as a flood of deep peace in the hearts of those who have come to know reality as it truly is through inquiry. What is required is to perform worship of that Self with a collected mind, so that the mind melts away through the power of a true love that is free of guile.

SRI NISARGADATTA MAHARAJ
(1471 – 1530)

1471. It is the doing as I tell you that will bring light, not my telling you.

1472. Giving attention to attention, aware of being aware. Affectionate awareness is the crucial factor that brings Reality into focus.

1473. Awareness is undivided; awareness is aware of itself.

1474. When this awareness turns upon itself, you may call it the Supreme State.

1475. What you need is to be aware of being aware.

1476. Be aware of being conscious and seek the source of consciousness.

1477. Awareness is unattached and unshaken. It is lucid, silent, peaceful, alert and unafraid, without desire and fear. Meditate on it as your true being.

1478. Awareness itself is all important, not the content of it. Deepen and broaden your awareness of yourself and all the blessings will flow.

1479. You are conscious. Hold on to it.

1480. The mind must learn that beyond the moving mind there is the background of awareness, which does not change. The mind must come to know the true Self and respect it and cease covering it up.

1481. The seer becomes conscious of himself as the seer.

1482. Mere knowledge is not enough; the knower must be known.

1483. To break the spell of the known the knower must be brought to the forefront.

1484. Forget the known, but remember that you are the knower. Don't be all the time immersed in your experiences.

1485. Meet yourself as the knower, apart from the known. Once you know yourself as pure being, the ecstasy of freedom is your own.

1486. Without the knowledge of the knower there can be no peace.

1487. To go beyond you must look away from the mind and its contents.

1488. Moods are in the mind and do not matter. Go within, go beyond. Cease being fascinated by the content of your consciousness.

1489. It is the nature of the mind to roam about. All you can do is to shift the focus of consciousness beyond the mind.

1490. The all-important word is 'try.' Allot enough time daily for sitting quietly and trying, just trying to go beyond the personality.

1491. What matters is the persistence with which you keep on returning to yourself.

1492. All you need to do is to try and try again.

1493. You just keep on trying until you succeed. If you persevere, there can be no failure. What matters supremely is sincerity, earnestness; you must really have had surfeit of being the person you are, now see the urgent need of being free of this unnecessary self-identification with a bundle of memories and habits. This steady resistance against the unnecessary is the secret of success.

1494. Maharaj: It is not a matter of easy, or difficult. You have no alternative. Either you try or you don't. It is up to you.

Questioner: I have tried many times and failed.

Maharaj: Try again. If you keep on trying, something may happen. But if you don't, you are stuck. You may know all the right words, quote the scriptures, be brilliant in your discussions and yet remain a bag of bones. Or you may be inconspicuous and humble, an insignificant person altogether, yet glowing with loving kindness and deep wisdom.

1495. The mind will rebel in the beginning, but with patience and perseverance it will yield and keep quiet.

1496. All our habits go against it and the task of fighting them is long and hard sometimes, but clear understanding helps a lot.

1497. When I met my Guru, he told me: "You are not what you take yourself to be. Find out what you are. Watch the sense 'I am', find your real Self." I obeyed him, because I trusted him. I did as he told me. All my spare time I would spend looking at myself in silence. And what a difference it made, and how soon! It took me only three years to realize my true nature. My Guru died soon after I met him, but it made no difference. I remembered what he told me and persevered.

1498. I used to sit for hours together, with nothing but the 'I am' in my mind and soon peace and joy and a deep all-embracing love became my normal state. In it all disappeared – myself, my Guru, the life I lived, the world around me. Only peace remained and unfathomable silence.

1499. You have only to look and see. Look at your Self, at your own being.

1500. Awareness is primordial; it is the original state, beginningless, endless, uncaused, unsupported, without parts, without change.

1501. All happiness comes from awareness. The more we are conscious, the deeper the joy.

1502. Awareness is the point at which the mind reaches out beyond itself into reality.

1503. At all times consciousness remains the same. To know it as it is, is realization and timeless peace.

1504. Do not undervalue attention. It means interest and also love.

1505. Give attention to the reality within you and it will come to light.

1506. Look at yourself, towards yourself, into yourself.

1507. Intelligence is the door to freedom and alert attention is the mother of intelligence.

1508. You are in bondage by inadvertence. Attention liberates.

1509. Look at yourself steadily – it is enough.

1510. Seek within. Your own Self is your best friend.

1511. The Self by its nature knows itself only.

1512. Being shines as knowing, knowing is warm in love. It is all one. You imagine separations and trouble yourself with questions.

1513. Being is consciousness.

1514. Establish yourself firmly in the awareness of 'I am.' This is the beginning and also the end of all endeavor.

1515. Why not turn away from the experience to the experiencer and realize the full import of the only true statement you can make: 'I am'?

1516. Separate the observed from the observer and abandon false identifications.

1517. Be true to your own Self, love your Self absolutely.

1518. You will be a fully awakened witness of the field of consciousness. But there should be no feelings and ideas to stand between you and the field.

1519. Maharaj: How do you go about finding anything? By keeping your mind and heart on it. Interest there must be and steady remembrance. To remember what needs to be remembered is the secret of success. You come to it through earnestness.

Questioner: Do you mean to say that mere wanting to find out is enough? Surely, both qualifications and opportunities are needed.

Maharaj: These will come with earnestness. What is supremely important is to be free from contradictions: the goal and the way must not be on different levels; life and light must not quarrel; behavior must not betray belief. Call it honesty, integrity, wholeness; you must not go back, undo, uproot, abandon the conquered ground. Tenacity of purpose and honesty in pursuit will bring you to your goal.

Questioner: Tenacity and honesty are endowments, surely! Not a trace of them I have.

Maharaj: All will come as you go on. Take the first step first. All blessings come from within. Turn within. 'I am' you know. Be with it all the time you can spare, until you revert to it spontaneously. There is no simpler and easier way.

1520. Be interested in yourself beyond all experience, be with yourself, love yourself; the ultimate security is found only in Self-knowledge. The main thing is earnestness. Be honest with yourself.

1521. Maharaj: Your own Self is your ultimate teacher. The outer teacher is merely a milestone. It is only your inner teacher that will walk with you to the goal, for he is the goal.

Questioner: The inner teacher is not easily reached.

Maharaj: Since he is in you and with you, the difficulty cannot be serious. Look within, and you will find him.

Questioner: When I look within, I find sensations and perceptions, thoughts and feelings, desires and fears, memories and expectations. I am immersed in this cloud and see nothing else.

Maharaj: That which sees all this, and the nothing too, is the inner teacher. He alone is, all else only appears to be. He is your own Self, your hope and assurance of freedom; find him and cling to him and you will be saved and safe.

1522. It is the person you imagine yourself to be that suffers, not you. Dissolve it in awareness. It is merely a bundle of memories and habits. From the awareness of the unreal to the awareness of your real nature there is a chasm which you will easily cross, once you have mastered the art of pure awareness.

1523. Who has not the daring will not accept the real even when offered. Unwillingness born out of fear is the only obstacle.

1524. Only the waking up is important.

1525. Meet your own Self. Be with your own Self, listen to it, obey it, cherish it, keep it in mind ceaselessly. You need no other guide.

1526. To become free, your attention must be drawn to the 'I am', the witness.

1527. Relax and watch the 'I am.'

1528. The awareness that you are will open your eyes to what you are. It is all very simple. First of all, establish a constant contact with your Self, be with yourself all the time. Into Self-awareness all blessings flow.

1529. Evil is the shadow of inattention. In the light of Self-awareness it will wither and fall off.

1530. Only what you discover through your own awareness, your own effort, will be of permanent use to you.

THE SUPREME YOGA
(1531 - 1569)

1531. It is by the action of consciousness becoming aware of itself that intelligence manifests itself, not when consciousness apprehends an inert object.

1532. The one Self perceives itself within itself as the infinite consciousness.

1533. This ocean of world-appearance can be crossed only when you are firmly established in supreme wisdom, when you see the Self with the Self alone, and when your intelligence is not diverted or colored by sense-perceptions.

1534. Without delay one should endeavor to see the Self.

1535. Contemplate the sole reality of consciousness for the cessation of repeated birth. Taste the pure consciousness, which is, in truth, the very essence of all that exists, by resolutely renouncing objectivity of consciousness (all the concepts and percepts) and contemplating the changeless consciousness which is infinite.

1536. Know that you are the essence of consciousness.

1537. Remain as pure consciousness without any disturbance in it.

1538. Be firmly established in this wisdom and discard the impure notion of ego-sense from your heart. When the pure heart contemplates the infinite space of consciousness, which is the source of all bliss and which is within easy reach of all, it rests in the Supreme Self.

1539. The mind should rest in pure consciousness as pure consciousness.

1540. Consciousness alone is the heart of all beings, not the piece of flesh which people call the heart!

1541. That Self or the infinite consciousness knows itself by itself; experiences itself in itself by itself.

1542. Now that you have lost the false characteristic of a mind, you exist as the supreme being or the infinite consciousness, freed from all limitation and conditioning.

1543. With my vision turned upon the Self, I rest in the Self.

1544. Infinite consciousness, which is devoid of concepts and extremely subtle, knows itself.

1545. Consciousness being its own object, is consciousness at all times.

1546. Abandon the habit of apprehending the objects with your mind. The knowers of THAT (Self) have seen what is worth seeing.

1547. It is the awareness in all that is sentient, it knows itself as its own object.

1548. This is the supreme meditation, this is the supreme worship: the continuous and unbroken awareness of the indwelling presence, inner light or consciousness.

1549. One should realize one's essential nature as pure consciousness. Thus does one attain liberation.

1550. The Self realizes the Self, the Self sees the Self on account of its own Self-luminous nature.

1551. It is only the Self that becomes aware of the Self.

1552. The consciousness is freed from the object. There is pure inner consciousness.

1553. Consciousness becomes conscious of its own consciousness; it cannot be realized otherwise.

1554. Only the Self knows the Self.

1555. Consciousness remains consciousness and is realized by consciousness.

1556. Consciousness shines as consciousness.

1557. Since there is neither a contradiction nor a division in consciousness it is Self-evident.

1558. Consciousness alone exists in consciousness.

1559. I abandoned all material and physical concepts and held on to the vision of pure consciousness.

1560. He who is enlightened sees not the diversity.

1561. I practiced concentration. I sat in the lotus-posture and remained as pure consciousness. I gathered all the rays of the mind which were dissipated over a thousand things and focused them on my own heart.

1562. The Self is its own object now and there is no other externalizing activity. Hence, it shines in itself as itself.

1563. The Self knows itself.

1564. You have heard all this, but you do not rest in the truth. Only by constant practice does this truth become fully established.

1565. His mind is at rest who enjoys observing or watching himself and is disinterested in external events and observations. When one's awareness is thus firmly held within oneself, the mind abandons its usual restlessness and flows towards wisdom.

1566. You are the seer. You are consciousness.

1567. Consciousness is conscious of itself as consciousness.

1568. The light of the enlightened itself is Self-awareness.

1569. Behold the light of consciousness within your Self by your Self.

1570. Turning one's purified awareness within on the witness as pure consciousness, one should gradually bring it to stillness and then become aware of the perfection of one's true nature.

1571. This has the nature of Self-awareness, since it is conscious of itself.

1572. They who rest on the Self that is consciousness, who have put away the outward, the imaginations of the ear and senses, and selfish personality, they verily, are free from the bonds and snares of the world, but not they who only meditate on what others have seen.

1573. Through intending the inner mind to it, gain the vision of the Self.

1574. The universal Self is witness of itself.

Please use the contact form on the seeseer.com website to let us know if reading The Seven Steps to Awakening was a good experience for you.

www.seeseer.com

LaVergne, TN USA
29 September 2010
198868LV00005B/110/P